D0619523

MILITARISM

The History of an International Debate
1861 — 1979

MILITARISM

The History of an International Debate
1861 — 1979

Volker R. Berghahn
Professor of History, University of Warwick

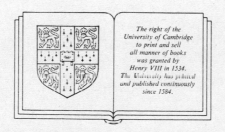

The right of the
University of Cambridge
to print and sell
all manner of books
was granted by
Henry VIII in 1534.
The University has printed
and published continuously
since 1584.

CAMBRIDGE UNIVERSITY PRESS

Cambridge

London   New York   New Rochelle

Melbourne   Sydney

ALBRIGHT COLLEGE LIBRARY

Published by the Press Syndicate of the University of Cambridge
The Pitt Building, Trumpington Street, Cambridge CB2 1RP
32 East 57th Street, New York, NY 10022, USA
296 Beaconsfield Parade, Middle Park, Melbourne 3206, Australia

© Berg Publishers Ltd. 1981

First published by Berg Publishers 1981
First paperback edition published by Cambridge University Press 1984

Printed in Great Britain at the
University Press, Cambridge

Library of Congress catalogue card number: 83–24072

British Library Cataloguing in Publication Data

Berghahn, Volker R.
Militarism: the history of an international debate, 1861–1979.
1. Militarism 2. Military history, Modern — 19th century
2. Military history, Modern — 20th century
I. Title
355′.0213   U21.2

ISBN 0 521 26905 9

LT

355
β497m

207978

Contents

11.95

Introduction

The growth and proliferation of historical and social science research since the Second World War has made it increasingly difficult to survey a particular area of academic work and to gauge how much ground has been covered in the evolution of a scholarly argument. This certainly appears to be true of a wide and important field which for a long time has attracted writers from very different backgrounds and disciplines and which is concerned with the role and position of the military in state and society. Large numbers of historians, sociologists, political scientists, peace researchers and psychologists have been preoccupied with what, after 1945, came to be known as civil-military relations and have grappled with the applicability or otherwise of the concept of militarism. There are numerous professional journals in the field.[1]* Several attempts have been made to compile comprehensive bibliographies of writings on the topic of militarism.[2] Not surprisingly, the volumes ran into thousands of titles.

These quantitative developments have not made it easier for all involved to see the wood for the trees. However, the fragmentation of social science research has also contributed to the growing difficulty of scholars to remain aware of what is going on across the fence on another academic patch. This also applies to information about the work of earlier generations. In these circumstances, it makes sense to pause from time to time in order to take stock of research in a particular field and to look back upon the meandering evolution of an argument. This at least is the idea behind the present volume which proposes to examine the history of the notion of militarism as a key concept of modern social science research — a concept which, to our knowledge, has never been treated comprehensively in this way.[3]

The subsequent chapters will therefore try to give a survey of the debate on militarism among historians, sociologists and other writers. It is a debate which has engaged a considerable number of powerful minds now for over a century. Some of them have approached the problem from the perspective of civil-military relations; others have been more interested in the mentalities and value systems of the military. Yet another group has been trying to interpret the role and function of the military against the background of a particular country's political economy. All these and other areas have attracted the theoretician, the social critic or the man of the broad sweep. At the other end of the spectrum, there have been those who prefer to take a magnifying-glass to the primary sources. The 1960s and 1970s especially saw the publication of a good deal of solid empirical work, and the history of a large variety of countries has been researched from at least one of the above-mentioned angles.[4] Of course, upon closer inspection, few of the empiricists have been satisified with the mere collation and presentation of their material. Many of them have, explicitly or implicitly, attempted to give their findings a more general relevance or even to assign them a place in the wider theoretical debate on the concept of militarism. As will be seen, few people hesitate to apply the term.

However, although the widespread usage of a concept may be seen to reflect its importance, there is no general agreement on its meaning. Worse, like imperialism, militarism is and always has been a word of political propaganda and polemic. Today East European countries accuse the West of being militaristic. Conversely, frequent warnings have been heard against a Red militarism. Up to the late 1940s, East and West were publicly united in their determination to prevent a rebirth of a German militarism. Two-thirds of the countries of Africa and more than half of the population of Latin America are governed today by regimes which many people would call militaristic. It might be argued that its frequent use in political propaganda has made the concept of militarism unsuitable for scholarship. Yet, if this were accepted, a good many other key words, including imperialism and fascism, would have to be excised from our vocabulary. Fortunately, there are many important works which evidently regard militarism as a meaningful analytical tool and merely wrestle with making it more meaningful and precise.

That we are very far from discarding the notion of militarism is also demonstrated by the fact that it appears in many established dictionaries and encyclopedias, even if definitions are far from uniform. Thus *The Shorter Oxford English Dictionary*, in taking over, almost verbatim, the version of the *Oxford English Dictionary* (OED), defines militarism as:[5] 'The spirit and tendencies of the professional soldier; the prevalence of military sentiment and ideals among a people; the tendency to regard military efficiency as the paramount interest of the state.' The OED of 1933 had included the following sentence which was taken out 40 years later:[6] 'The political conditions characterised by the predominance of the military class in government or administration.' *The Encyclopedia Americana* defines the term as being 'applied to the policy of giving exceptional emphasis to military preparedness, exalting military virtues and relying on force in international relations'.[7] The French *Grand Larousse* circumscribes militarism as the 'exaggerated preponderance of the military element in a nation; a political system which bases itself upon the army; sentiment, doctrine of those who favour this preponderance of the army.'[8] The *Dizionario Enciclopedico Italiano* speaks of the 'prevalence, in a state or class, of a military spirit: [e.g.] Prussian militarism.'[9] A shorter Spanish encyclopedia writes that militarism represents the 'predominance of the military element in the government of the State',[10] whereas the widely used West German *Brockhaus* speaks of the 'predominance of military forms, thought patterns and objectives in state, politics and society'.[11] The East German *Marxistisch-Leninistisches Wörterbuch der Philosophie,* on the other hand, sees it as a 'reactionary and aggressive system of domination and organization in social orders based on exploitation' in which 'economic, social and cultural life is subjected to a military clique which views military force and war in particular as the main instrument for the realization of an aggressive policy'.[12] The *Sovietskaia istoricheskaia enciklopedia* finally describes militarism as a 'closed system of economics, politics and ideology' resulting in a 'policy of military expansion of the exploiter state with the aim of preparing wars of conquest and of repressing the resistance of the exploited masses within that state'.[13]

In different ways, all these definitions will re-emerge in subsequent chapters. However, this book is not intended to provide fresh empirical material in support of any of these definitions. It is therefore not to be compared with the *History of Militarism* written by Alfred Vagts some forty years ago.[14] Nor is it concerned with the problem of war in human society as it has been studied from divergent perspectives, but again by reference to historical material by such authors as Quincy Wright, John U. Nef or David Singer.[15] The aim of this volume is rather to examine the debate surrounding the concept of militarism since it made its first appearance in the nineteenth century. It is concerned with other authors' arguments, many of whom — it should be pointed out — presented their evidence from a critical and anti-militarist, though not necessarily anti-military position. Nevertheless, this study tries to go beyond simply recounting what these authors have been saying on the subject. It is also concerned with the genesis and development of militarism as an analytical tool in relation to discussions about the evolution of modern society.

Consequently, the following chapters range not only across divergent disciplines, but also across a variety of countries and ideological frontiers. No claim is made that the analysis is all-inclusive, although it is hoped that the main currents and turning-points have been identified. Nor was it possible for the author to be equally at home in widely differing fields and national histories. Yet if the analysis is not always finely balanced, this is primarily due to the fact that its foci were inevitably determined by the territory on which the debate on militarism happened to be moving. As the German historian Hans Herzfeld observed in 1956, the pre-1945 discussion of the concept 'was almost exclusively fought out in the arena of German history'.[16]

It will be seen that this was an exaggeration resulting from the narrow perspective of the generation of German historians to which Herzfeld belonged. Nevertheless, the German case did assume a prominent place in the debate and this will unavoidably be reflected in the first chapters of this study. In fact, Germany's militarism came to be seen by many as a paradigm and hence caused considerable argument among scholars both inside and outside Central Europe. And even when people wrote on other cases of militarism, the German example was, in one way or another, often at the back of their minds. It was only after 1945 that a marked shift of emphasis took place in this respect, at least among non-historians. There were first of all those Anglo-Saxon sociologists and political scientists who began to turn their attention to the position of the military in the so-called New Nations of the Third World. Almost simultaneously, other scholars in the West started to raise the question of whether an 'advanced' industrial nation like the United States ought to be called militaristic. These were interesting developments not only in themselves, but also because the contrast between developing and developed countries has in effect provided the framework in which the entire debate has implicitly always been conducted.

It is important to emphasize these unspoken assumptions, as not all of the writers whose views will be examined below have been conscious of this broader societal context. This is true in particular of those who were either concerned to describe the outward features of militarism or who saw the problem primarily as one of the role of the military in political decision-making. Nevertheless, most authors have made certain assumptions about the societies with reference to which they raised the problem of militarism. The question which we shall therefore have to ask is: what are the socio-economic and political structures which an author presumes to exist in his or her case study and, relatedly, what is the contemporary ideological context in which these presuppositions are rooted?

The approach of the following chapters should now be clear: it is not to do a demolition job on previous writings in order to erect a new theory of militarism upon the rubble of earlier work. The method is rather to try to identify the 'thread' which has run through the debate of the past 100 or so years and to see if it is possible to construct from this material a typology of militarism which may form the explicit framework of future investigations into the subject. It was therefore also sensible to adhere to a broadly chronological approach which starts from the first appearance of the concept in the nineteenth century and takes the story up to the First World War in Chapter I. The interwar period saw the growth of military apparatuses and para-military organisations which led to much argument among academics and non-academics to be recounted in Chapter II. Since Prussia-Germany and Japan appeared to be the prime examples of militaristic systems prior to 1945, a lively discussion restarted after the Second World War concerning the nature and origins of these particular militarisms which will be examined in Chapter III. The next chapter then deals with studies of the role of the military in Third World countries which became a major industry from the 1950s onwards, especially in the United States. It was overshadowed only from the late 1960s onwards by a preoccupation with the apparent militarization of different spheres of life in the developed industrial countries; accordingly, Chapter V will try to throw some light on the significance of the debate surrounding the so-called Military-Industrial Complex in the United States and its Soviet equivalent. Finally, Chapter VI represents an attempt to differentiate between types of militarism. This typology is partly derived from the previous chapters, but also from a case study which looks at Nazi Germany as a militaristic system.

The book arose from an anthology on militarism which I edited several years ago for a West German publisher and which contained contributions to the debate by such authors as Herbert Spencer, Otto Hintze, Karl Liebknecht, Harold Lasswell and others.[17] I discovered at the time that there was nothing comparable in English to the longer introduction which I wrote for this anthology. The expansion of the theme into a monograph made it necessary for me to venture into areas of research, such as Japanese history or the massive work on the Military-Industrial Complex, in which I could never claim to be a specialist. I am therefore grateful to a number of colleagues who drew my attention to various inaccuracies and misinterpretations in the draft manuscript. I particularly benefited from the criticisms of Professor Morris Janowitz, Dr. Tim Mason, Professor Eiji Ohno, Mr. Richard

Storry and Dr. Jay Winter. Any remaining omissions and errors of substance or judgement are, of course, entirely my own responsibility.

Notes

1   Thus the 1979 issue of the *War and Society Newsletter,* a bibliographical reference periodical edited by Geoffrey Best, Wilhelm Deist, Andrew Wheatcroft and Samuel Williamson, now monitors some forty-six professional journals in the field.

2   See, e.g., M. Thompson, 'Militarism 1969. A Survey of World Trends.' *Peace Research News* 5 (1968), pp. 1–96.

3   Major reference works such as the *International Encyclopedia of the Social Sciences* or the *Lexikon Historischer Grundbegriffe* have an entry under 'militarism', but they are either rather brief or focus on the development of the concept in one country during a limited period.

4   The debate on Latin American militarism has been particularly extensive and detailed. See below pp. 74ff.

5   *The Shorter Oxford English Dictionary,* Oxford 1973, p.1323.

6   *The Oxford English Dictionary,* Oxford 1933, p.438.

7   *The Encyclopedia Americana,* Vol. 19, New York 1968, p.59.

8   *Grand Larousse,* Vol. 7, Paris 1963, p.361.

9   *Dizionario Enciclopedico Italiano,* Vol. 7, Rome 1957, p.759.

10 *Diccionario Enciclopédico Abreviado,* Vol. 5, Madrid 1957, p.891.

11 *Brockhaus Enzyklopädie,* Vol. 12, Wiesbaden 1971, p.560.

12 *Marxistisch-Leninistisches Wörterbuch der Philosophie,* Vol. 2, Leipzig 1969, p.724f.

13 *Sovietskaia istoricheskaia enciklopedia,* Vol. 9, Moscow 1966, p.436.

14 A. Vagts, *A History of Militarism,* London 1938.

15 Q. Wright, *A Study of War,* 2 vols., Chicago 1942; J. U. Nef, *War and Human Progress,* New York 1963; D. Singer, ed., *Quantitative International Politics. Insights and Evidence,* New York 1968. Singer's Michigan Project was, in the first instance, concerned with the collection of statistical data on wars and military conflicts in the modern period. Nef's focus is on Western Industrial Civilization and modern warfare since the fifteenth century. Wright deals with the nature, conditions of and controls on, war. He mentions the problem of 'militarization' briefly and is inclined, in a Liberal tradition, to associate militarism with feudal societies.

16 H. Herzfeld, 'Zur neueren Literatur über das Heeresproblem in der deutschen Geschichte.' *Vierteljahrshefte für Zeitgeschichte* 4 (1956), p.370.

17 V. R. Berghahn, ed., *Militarismus,* Cologne 1975.

I   The Debate Prior to 1914

According to the German historian Werner Conze the term 'militarism' first appeared in the *Memoirs* of Madame de Chastenay in 1816/18.[1]* But the date is uncertain and the word does not appear to have been used during the next 45 years until 1861 when it was mentioned in Pierre Proudhon's *La guerre et la paix*.[2] In 1864, he applied it again in his essay *De la capacité politique des classes ouvrières*.[3] During the same year the term also emerges in the Central European journal *Deutsche Jahrbücher für Politik und Literatur*,[4] as well as in English. By 1869, 'militarism' had found its way into a French encyclopedia, a year later into a German one.[5] It was thus established as a neologism in France and Central Europe and spread to other countries from there.

It is more difficult to decide what those who first coined the term actually meant by it. De Chastenay apparently thought of it in the context of the regime of Napoleon I. Proudhon, by contrast, linked it with military conflict and intended to describe by it an interpretation of history which favoured the idea of war as an activator of man's best moral energies. To him — that fighter for a just and civilized society — such a view was of course utterly repulsive. Nevertheless, it is interesting how he saw militarism as belonging to an autocratic phase of human history which, following a complete transformation of society, would eventually be replaced by a regime of liberty and economic equality. Three years later, in 1864, he used the term in a more restrictive sense to describe the military aspect of the centralized Belgian monarchy. At the same time he saw it in the context of the financial burdens imposed on the population by large modern armies.

Still, whether Proudhon saw militarism as a system antagonistic to a socialist-pacifist society or, alternatively, to his world without oppressive government, it is clear that he was in effect writing about a problem which had preoccupied philosophers and political commentators for the previous 200 years or more. We may have had militaristic regimes in the ancient world[6] or in the Middle Ages;[7] but it was not until the seventeenth century that people began to show a political or academic interest in the position of the military in the emergent nation states of the modern period. Hans Herzfeld, one of the foremost historians of this problem, discovered the origins of the debate on militarism in England and linked it to the Glorious Revolution of 1688 when, as he put it, 'the modern English state was born with its fundamental predominance of the civilian element over the military one in public affairs'.[8] He continued that, although the Bill of Rights of 1689 was more 'the product of a fear of tyranny than of a conscious opposition to militarism', it was nevertheless at this moment that a basic principle of modern liberalism and democracy began to assert itself. That the decision of the late seventeenth century was not quite so clear-cut and that, with the experience of Cromwell behind them, the relationship between the civilian government and the military continued to agitate contemporaries in England is evidenced by the publication, in 1697, of two books whose titles give the story away: John Trenchard's *An Argument Showing That A Standing Army Is Inconsistent With A Free Government And Absolutely Destructive To The Constitution Of The English Monarchy* and Andrew Fletcher's *A Discourse Concerning Militias And Standing Armies With Relation To The Past And Present Governments of Europe And of England In Particular*.

Trenchard would have found it difficult, if not impossible, to win his 'Argument' in the countries of the European Continent where absolutism had been gaining the upper hand over representative assemblies. The rise of absolutism was accompanied by the growth of large-scale military organisations which buttressed princely power. Across the Atlantic, the problem of the relationship between 'free government' and military power was also perceived by the authors of the American Declaration of Independence. They accused the King of militaristic tendencies because he had maintained 'among us, in times of peace, Standing Armies without the consent of our legislatures' and had tried 'to render the Military independent of, and superior to, the Civil power'.[9] The outcome of the War of Independence established the 'civilian principle' to which these words allude also in the United States of America. France and Central Europe were less fortunate and it is from there that the most persistent criticism of the military system of absolutism can be heard. Charles de Montesquieu was worried both by the mounting financial burdens as well as the size of armaments and by the isolation of the military from the citizens. His famous concept of the separation of powers is also reflected in his demand that, under a monarchical system, civilian and military offices should not be held by one and the same person.[10] Only under a Republican regime whose citizens are, in an external emergency, at the same time the defenders of the Fatherland would the dangers inherent in a combination of such offices disappear. Jean Jacques Rousseau, above all, idealized the notion of a militia of free citizens who would ultimately be deployed in the struggle against the mercenary forces of absolutist tyrants. In Germany, Immanuel Kant and Johann Gottlieb Fichte became outspoken critics of standing armies as threats to peace and economic prosperity, whereas Carl von Clausewitz, in his famous study, was more inclined to view the problems in terms of the proper subordination of military demands to political considerations. Overwhelmingly the problem of the military organization of society was seen at this time against the background of two competing political systems among which representative government would eventually overcome and supersede princely absolutism.

When the American historian Alfred Vagts later argued that militarism is 'not the opposite of pacifism; its true counterpart is civilianism',[11] he was in fact referring to a view which had established itself in the Anglo-Saxon world well before the twentieth century. Militarism was seen to obtain wherever and whenever military considerations exerted a decisive influence on civilian government. It was perceived as obstructing the development of representative institutions. It was the negative image of the political system that had taken root in England and the United States in the eighteenth century. We emphasize this particular tradition of thought not only because of its relevance to the debate in the present century, but also because it focuses so prominently on political institutions. On the other hand, it does adopt an evolutionist view of history in so far as militarism was widely held to be doomed and to be replaced by a civilian order. Thus 'Progress' — that all-pervasive idea of the early nineteenth century — was believed to be at work also in the field of civil-military relations and the realm of military politics. There are very few references to the socio-economic framework within which the transition was supposed to occur. To the extent that economic arguments were advanced by Kant and others, they tended to criticize large military establishments as wasteful and parasitic. But rarely did they go beyond a general statement of this kind.

It was Claude Henri de Rouvroy Comte de Saint-Simon and his followers who began to transcend the confines of politics and constitutions.[12] Their vision was that of a harmonious society of industrial producers in which military power would be superfluous. Saint-Simon, in his famous *Political Parable*, classified France's 'marshals' among those whom he regarded as dispensable relics of the ancien regime. Above all, the Saint-Simoneans developed the notion, in different versions soon to be found in other contemporary writings, that the advent of a society based on industry and commerce would once and for all also remove the problem which the existence of the military had been causing in earlier generations. In Victorian Britain, Free Trade and economic development were seen as the best antidote to war and heavy armaments expenditure, with Richard Cobden being one of the most ardent advocates of this idea. In Central Europe Wilhelm Schulz-Bodmer, a constitutional lawyer, similarly saw economic reform rather than constitutional change as an alternative to what he called '*Militär-herrschaft*'.[13]

By the time 'militarism' became established in political language, two major strands can be discerned within the critique of military organization and its effect upon civilian society, i.e. those analysts who saw it in a political and constitutional framework and those who examined it as a socio-economic problem. Both approaches shared a common vision of a progressive movement towards an age in which armies would at least be closely controlled, if not abolished altogether.

When Proudhon first used the term 'militarism' in the 1860s, he applied it, as we have seen, in both senses, thus contributing to a definitional muddle which was to last for the next 100 years and which will be traced in subsequent chapters. On the one hand, he identified it with a centralized type of political system; on the other hand, he regarded it as an obstacle to the achievement of a social order which was pacific and economically just. This confusion was compounded in the late 1860s when the concept of militarism was picked up by Catholic particularists in Central Europe as a polemical weapon against the hegemonic aspirations of Protestant Prussia. It was through this propaganda in the German South and in the Rhineland that the term was popularised. But almost inevitably it lost what little precision it had by then acquired in the process.

A good example of this use of the concept is a pamphlet by Georg Pachtler, a Jesuit monk, which he published under the pseudonym Annuarius Osseg.[14] His 'European Militarism' was identical with systems whose *raison d'être* was organization for war. To him the centralizing tendencies of his time, rearmament to the utmost and the mobilization of all national resources for the purposes of maintaining a large army were essential features of a type of modern militarism to be observed in the 1860s in both Bismarckian Prussia and in Napoleonic France. Pachtler even went so far as to predict a time when, because of the spreading of the militarist principle, Europe would become 'one huge garrison' geared to the application of force against opponents at home and neighbours abroad. It was a pessimistic argument which was absent from liberal writings and which was to gain wider currency only after the turn of the century. In the view of Philipp Wasserburg, another Catholic writer, militarism was 'the result of a political (dis)order which interferes with interstate relations which are governed by the rule of international law'.[15] Unlike Pachtler who, writing during Bismarck's *Kulturkampf*, appears to have been more interested in the internal aspect of militarism, Wasserburg was most concerned with the threat the military posed, in his view at least, to international peace and order. Both authors were united in their opinion that Prussia was the embodiment of militarism. Her continued rise was therefore to be resisted. All in all it seems that the Central European debate of the 1870s was too charged politically to facilitate the beginnings of an analytical clarification of the concept of militarism.

It was easier for a scholar living at safe distance from Prussia on the other side of the Channel to take a more sober look at how militarism might be most appropriately defined. This man was Herbert Spencer, one of the fathers of modern sociology. In the mid-1880s he advanced what appears to have been the first systematic analysis of militarism, although he preferred to call it an examination of a 'militant type of society'.[16] This was a society 'in which all men fit for fighting act in concert against other societies'. More than that: 'Besides the direct aid of all who can fight, there is given the indirect aid of all who cannot fight.' From this he concluded: 'Given two societies of which the members are all either warriors or those who supply the needs of warriors, and other things equal, supremacy will be gained by that in which the efforts of all are most effectually combined.' One result of this pressure is, according to Spencer, that the 'development of the militant type involves the close binding of the society into a whole'. Individualism will be unacceptable. The citizen's life 'is not his own, but is at the disposal of his society'. In short, 'under the militant type the individual is owned by the State', which in turn requires strong controls and 'a system of centralization'. Seen in a different light, the 'process of militant organization' is tantamount to a 'process of regimentation which, primarily taking place in the army, secondarily affects the whole community'. Ultimately, all aspects of public life would have to be supervised and enforced.

Another consequence of the imperatives of a 'militant type of society' was 'that organizations other than those forming parts of the State-organization are wholly or partially repressed'. Finally there was the fact that 'a society of the militant type tends to evolve a self-sufficient sustaining organization; with its political autonomy there goes what we may call an economic autonomy'. To Spencer it was also self-evident that this type of social organization required a particular type of human being:

> Making success in war the highest glory, they are led to identify goodness with bravery and strength. Revenge becomes a sacred duty with them; and acting at home on the law of retaliation which they act on abroad, they similarly, at home as abroad, are ready to sacrifice others to self: their sympathies, continually deadened during war, cannot be active during peace. They must have patriotism which regards the triumph of their society as the supreme end of action; they must possess the loyalty whence flows obedience to authority; and that they may be obedient they must have abundant faith. With faith in authority and consequent readiness to be directed, naturally goes relatively little power of initiation. The habit of seeing everything officially controlled fosters the belief that official control is everywhere needful.

It is not too difficult to see what kind of society Spencer had in mind. But to make certain that he was not misunderstood, he proceeded to give a number of examples, and the rest of the chapter then discusses the 'militant societies' of Dahomé, Sparta, Egypt, Prussia, the Incas and Russia.

Next, Spencer postulated that these societies contrasted starkly with another type. He argued that it was not a socialist or communist one which also involved, albeit 'in another form, the principle of compulsory cooperation'.[17] Rather it was a regime which defended the citizen's individuality instead of sacrificing it to society. In fact, 'defence of his individuality becomes the society's essential duty'. Spencer called this type of society 'industrial'. It was a social organization 'in which life, liberty and property are secure and all interests justly regarded'. Because it was not geared to war, but to industrial production and peaceful economic interchange, there was no need in it 'for a despotic controlling agency'. Such controls as would be required would be exercised 'by an appointed agency for ascertaining and executing the average will; and a representative agency is the one best fitted for doing this'. This would be the body in which divergent interests would be conciliated and equitable adjustments made, while a general consensus about the fundamental principles upon which this type of society rested would be preserved. Any administration required would be decentralized and narrow in scope. On the other hand, Spencer's industrial type of society was not an egalitarian one: 'For when, the struggle for existence between societies by war having ceased, there remains only the industrial struggle for existence, the final survival and spread must be on the part of those societies which produce the largest number of the best individuals — individuals best adapted for life in the industrial state.'

Enough has been said, it is hoped, to appreciate that Spencer's industrial society was built along the lines of classical liberal doctrine, fortified by a heavy dose of Social Darwinism.[18] One last important point has to be made concerning his system: it is obvious that the militant and industrial forms of social organization represented ideal types in a Weberian sense. No-one was more conscious than Spencer of the fact that reality was much more blurred. The advantage of his approach, he said, was that 'having contemplated the society ideally organized for war, we shall be prepared to recognise in real societies the characters which war has brought about'. And this is what his subsequent analysis tried to do. He is therefore also quite willing to admit that 'militant societies' can be engaged in industry. But, he added, they are 'industrially occupied, not industrially organized'. Thus the 'mode of organization of the labourers' is tendentially different. Conversely, industrially organized systems, coexisting as they do with warrior societies, are vulnerable to attack from the outside and hence have to set aside a certain amount of human effort for defence.

Yet 'whereas in the militant type the demand for corporate action is intrinsic, such demand for corporate action as continues in the industrial type is mainly extrinsic — is called for by those aggressive traits of human nature which chronic warfare has fostered, and may gradually diminish as, under enduring peaceful life, these decrease'. Spencer predicted this process would result in a loss of autonomy and in greater international cooperation. In short, 'with the spread of industrialism . . . the tendency is towards the breaking down of the divisions between nationalities and the running through them of a common organization: if not under a single government, then under a federation of governments.'

Although he is vague about how this 'spread of industrialism' started, he points out that it arose 'by modification of pre-existing structures'. He sees the emergence of more distant industrial forms as a long-drawn-out process, but leaves no doubt that a universal industrial type of society is bound to replace the militant one in due course. To this extent, Spencer was and remained a firm believer in the nineteenth-century Idea of Progress. It would be easy to expose a number of flaws in his treatise, especially in the light of developments in the twentieth century. On the other hand, he formulated questions which were to be debated in later decades, even if few subsequent authors have explicitly referred to him. His overall framework of analysis will therefore have to be borne in mind.

One of those who did draw on Spencer directly was Otto Hintze, an eminent constitutional historian of Wilhelmine Germany, who took another look at the scheme in 1906.[19] Hintze was not all happy with what he found. To begin with, he objected to Spencer's methodology of devising a general framework and then, as he put it, to scavenge history and ethnology in search of supporting evidence. This 'non-genetic' approach had done violence to live cultural entities and in the end had brought to light no more than 'obvious trivialities'. After this swipe at sociology as a discipline which historians loved to administer in his time, Hintze produced his own 'genetic' interpretation of the development of societies. Starting from the fundamental hypothesis that 'all state organization was originally military organization, or-ganization of war', he took the Germanic nations as his illustration. However, the postulated identity of state organization and organization for war was not supposed to imply that these nations were 'militant' or, to use Hintze's term, 'militaristic'. The societies which emerged on the European Continent from the rubble of the Roman Empire had passed, he wrote, through *three* great epochs. Only the last of these, beginning towards the end of the fifteenth century, was the 'epoch of militarism'.

The dividing line between the earlier — feudal — and the subsequent militaristic age was, according to Hintze, provided by 'an important institution. . .: the ordnance companies of Charles VII of France'. They were 'from the standpoint of political organization. . . something new: the first standing army in Europe based on the King's exclusive sovereign right to make war'. It was an 'epoch-making' innovation on the Continent which Charles the Bold of Burgundy and Maximilian of Austria were to imitate. No less significant was that the emergence of monarchical state entities was parallelled by the creation of militias. What is more: 'The advance in the art of war and military organization which made possible the development of militarism on the Continent derived from the peasant militias', with the Swiss becoming 'the great teachers of all nations' in military tactics. They forced the princes into more effective ways of organizing their own military power; their counter-moves in turn generated interstate rivalries, transforming feudalism in the process which hitherto had been geared to 'prosperity and order, rather than to military might'. A new system was born in which power politics and the struggle for supremacy became the over-riding concerns. In this way, Continental armies became 'the very backbone of the new centralized greater state'. It was the absence of external threats which enabled England to take a different road. For she did not need standing armies, only a navy. Hintze went on that this difference could equally well be expressed in political terms:

'Absolutism and militarism go together on the Continent just as do self-government and militia in England'. In other words, the differing ways in which political and military organizations developed on either side of the Channel 'lies in the difference in their foreign situations'.

Hintze's point concerning the weight of military geography can hardly be overemphasized not only by comparison with Spencer's argument, but also vis-à-vis the Marxist interpretation of militarism which will be discussed in a moment. If he was critical of Spencer, he was even more so of the Marxists. Consequently he lost no time in refuting, at the beginning of his essay, the 'one-sided, exaggerated and therefore false' view that class struggles were the 'driving force of history'. Conflicts between nations, he added, have been 'far more important, and throughout the ages pressure from without has been the determining influence on internal structure'.

His refutation of Marxism and of the idea of the primacy of domestic politics apart, Hintze was also deeply sceptical of Spencer's notion that a liberal-industrial type of society would gradually replace the monarchical-militaristic one. It was correct, he wrote, that tensions would always exist between a representative Republican system and a large standing army, 'for the army by its nature demands a monarch at its head, while the President of the Republic is by nature a civilian'. Hence 'militarism and republics do not get along too well together' and the monarchical element will continue to 'cling to modern militarism, even where it has vanished from the constitution of the state itself'. However, Hintze did not see this situation in terms of a simple one-way threat. The introduction of universal military service, he argued, had alleviated some of the pressure on Republican systems while, conversely, creating problems for monarchical regimes.

Were these various tensions ever likely to become so serious as to cause an explosion of the respective system? Hintze did not think so. On the contrary, he believed that the militia principle would develop side-by-side with professional armies and that nothing would reinforce this trend more than the increasing globalism of power politics. Colonial empires, as he thought the British case demonstrated, required a type of army different from that available to the states of the European Continent. Just as the latter were becoming colonizing powers, it was not inconceivable to Hintze that British institutions would incline towards those of the Continent. In short, with the advent of mass warfare, on the one hand, and of colonial and naval expansion, on the other, 'England would be infused with something of the spirit of militarism, while the Continent would edge in the direction of a militia and navy'.

It may be true, he concluded, that land power and sea power reflected the different interests of divergent social classes and that the former was more likely to be supported by conservative-agrarian elements as opposed to the progressive commercial and industrial ethos of a navy. Nevertheless, once traditional European power politics became enlarged as result of Europe's participation in global politics, the above-mentioned peculiarities of individual states would weaken. 'The opposition between land powers and sea powers, between peoples that govern themselves and peoples that are governed from above will become less and less rigid and obvious.'

The implication of this was that Spencer's prediction of the future was quite wrong: the militaristic and the industrial type of society would 'probably experience not a sharpening of their differences, but a gradual blending and increasing similarity of institutions'. Nor was peace likely to prevail. On the contrary, 'in the foreseeable future, matters will remain as they have been throughout history: the form and the spirit of the state's organization will not be determined solely by economic and social relations and clashes of interests, but primarily by the necessities of defense and offense, that is by the organization of the army and of warfare'. Hintze's view was thus ultimately a pessimistic one — or 'realistic', as he would probably have called it. In this respect he merely voiced the feelings of his age after the turn of the century. Presumably he was confirmed in his expectation of the persistence of militarism and international violence by his study of modern bureaucracy, a field in which he made another major contribution to research.[20] This research led him to believe that centralization and, as he put it in his 1906 essay, 'bureaucratism' would merely reinforce the militaristic tendencies of the twentieth century; militarism, as he had defined it, would turn towards the outside.

For a conservative German professor it was perhaps possible to contemplate this prospect with detached equanimity. Most of his more liberal and/or pacifist contemporaries, on the other hand, not only found Hintze's neglect of the internal effects of militarism unacceptable, but were also appalled by the ever-growing influence of the military at home and abroad. More particularly it had become clear by the 1890s that universal conscription, which critics at the beginning of the century expected to exert a 'civilizing' influence on the army, had for all practical purposes resulted in the opposite: if the Prusso-German experience was anything to go by, universal military service had led to the militarization of the civilian sphere. After all, at the turn of the century the solid burgher scrambling for a commission in the reserve officer corps was no longer just a satirical figure. In Central

Europe at least many people accorded the status of a human being only to a man in uniform.

This irked a pacifist academic, Ludwig Quidde, so much that in 1893 he published a book on the problem of militarism in Wilhelmine Germany.[21] 'The peculiar position of militarism', he wrote, 'is rooted in the fact that the largest part of the male population is drafted into the Army for a number of years and that even thereafter the Army does not permit him to return in complete freedom to his profession.'[22] The effect of this was that military values had come to infiltrate civilian life and were being furthered by a variety of associations. In assessing the impact of this process especially on the propertied and educated middle classes, Quidde concluded that militarism had a 'corrupting' influence on society. Ultimately, he added, the spirit of the entire nation would be affected, above all in its 'development towards a free society and in its ability to use its liberty'.[23] Moreover, it would be 'hampered in its economic efficiency'. In Quidde's view, militarism suppressed individuality and was destructive of any ideas of democratically organized institutions. And last but not least, militarism would help to popularize the notion that war was a legitimate means of politics and an important factor of cultural advancement.

Quidde's anti-militarist moral commitment pervaded the pages of his book no less than his pessimism about the future. He had written his indictment against the background of the 1893 Army Bill, and the outcome of that political struggle demonstrated all too clearly that the critics of the Prusso-German military state were on the defensive.[24] Their position was further weakened by the inconsistencies of those among the critics of Wilhelmine society who pilloried the old-fashioned Prussian militarism and argued for transcending it by means of a policy of liberal imperialism whose democratic dynamic would crack up the traditional structures.[25] One writer, Carl Bleibtreu, even went to the extreme of extolling war and violence as a means of destroying the petrified positions of the Prusso-German military state.[26]

Although similar currents of thought also existed in the Western world in the decade before 1914, the nexus between the original civilian-liberal impetus behind the criticism of the military was never ruptured there in quite the same way as in Central Europe. A good example of this unadulterated liberal criticism is Joseph D. Miller's article which appeared in 1900 in Benjamin O. Flower's journal *Arena*.[27] Like Quidde, Miller was not so much concerned with the cost of standing armies as with the 'spirit of militarism' which he believed to be 'always on the side of reaction — always allied with the non-progressive and anti-liberal movements of the time'. He also took a determined stand against war and, rather overemotionally perhaps, against military men in general whom he called 'the Acephala among the human species'. Again like Quidde, he was convinced that militarism had a corrupting influence on society and voiced the fear that the American political system was also becoming exposed to it: 'However institutions preserve the outward garb of democracy, the Republic is slowly shaping itself to empire'. The connection between the drive for empire and the militarization of Republican life is elaborated in another passage in which he maintained:

> The spirit of militarism develops an unconscious hypocrisy, tending to obscure the real distinction of the rights of the weaker. We prate about "our rights" in the Philippines — "our right" to govern the Filipinos. Now it must be admitted that however little amenable men are to reason they are even less so to force. Then why not send 65,000 missionaries instead of soldiers to persuade the Filipinos that it is our "right" to govern them and that it is right for them to yield? The only reason we do not do so is because our talk of rights in such connection is shameless cant.

Although Miller had thus established an interesting link between late nineteenth-century imperialism and the rise of militarism, he did not go so far as to connect these two phenomena with American capitalism. To him, as to most good liberals of the time, 'industrialism and militarism are antagonistic'. Miller shared the view of economists like Joseph Schumpeter who postulated that capitalist industrialism was essentially peaceful and pacific.[28] What led to a perversion of this system and precipitated expansionist drives were, to use Schumpeter's term, 'atavistic' relics of a pre-industrial age preserved by the existence of warrior castes in modern society. In a similar vein, the British economist John A. Hobson may be seen not only as a foremost theoretician of imperialism whose writings influenced many authors on the subject, including Lenin, but also of militarism.[29] He, too, adhered to the view that there was nothing inherent in capitalism which stood in the way of ridding it of certain 'maladjustments' which had become manifest in the late nineteenth century. It was only logical that he should include the military among his group of social 'parasites' who had helped to acquire and maintain a burdensome colonial empire.

This was also the position of the philosopher and historian Guglielmo Ferrero who, writing from the perspective of his native 'backward' Italy, pulished his *Il Militarismo* in 1898, followed in 1902 by an expanded and modified translation into English.[30] The volume was dedicated to the founder and president of the first Italian Peace Society and was intended to be Ferrero's contribution 'to the grand work of pacifying civilized nations' in order to avoid the disaster of a general European war. Written from the point of view of an Italian Liberal and pervaded by a progressive teleology, the author put forward an analysis of the evolution of human society from a premodern stage in which wars had been inevitable and necessary to solve the problem of scarcity of capital, land and men to a stage of a 'mechanical-industrial civilization' such as existed in Britain 'where militarism is reduced to a minimum'. For Ferrero, peace was the 'advance towards justice, a desire for more liberal, equitable, wiser and less tyrannical government, and the peace movement represented 'one of the phases of the general progress towards liberty and justice in modern life'.

This modern society which was emerging in the West would be based on the 'development of work and consumption', whereas the old world had lived on pillage and conquest. It was apparently through the influence of Gaetano Mosca that Ferrero, moreover, came to see this transition as one which would change the relationship between divergent social groups:

> In the past nearly the whole responsibility of the work whereon the life of society depended was left to the ignorant peasant and humble artisan, compelled by force to provide the leisure of their ignorant and stupid masters with pleasures. Nowadays, on the contrary, the ruling class collaborates with the masses in working, and although it is frequently overpaid and often squanders the people's strength in creating unreal wealth, nevertheless it notably enhances the universal activity. England, Germany, America, and, in a minor degree, France and Italy — all civilized nations, in short — are no longer governed by oligarchies of idle sybarites, but by social groups who direct, more or less efficiently, the work of society. Owing to this change, it was possible that between societies which for thirty centuries had not ceased for an instance to persecute one another with wars, a sudden desire for peace should grow up . . . it arose principally from the fact that since the ruling class ceased to acquire wealth by brigandage, seizing it forcibly from other nations and classes, war lost its essential function and commenced to grow repugnant.

It is interesting that Ferrero thought Germany to be less bellicose than France although it was logical for him to adopt this view, once he had tied the decline of militarism to the rise of industrialism.

There is finally a book by Norman Angell, a British businessman, which may be seen to represent an amalgam of various liberal positions on the subject of militarism mentioned above. 'Angellism', as it came to be known, was Spencerism, Cobdenism, Hobsonianism all thrown together in a peripatetic treatise. Originally published in 1909 as a pamphlet under the title *Europe's Optical Illusion*, Angell's ideas attracted considerable attention, especially in the Anglo-Saxon world.[31] The book ran through several impressions and a revised and expanded version appeared in 1910 entitled *The Great Illusion. A Study of the Relation Of Military Power In Nations To Their Economic and Social Advantage*[32]. By 1912, the volume had been translated into more than ten European and non-European languages. Although extremely wide-ranging in historical place and time, its fundamental point was a very simple one: that the statesmen and peoples of Europe would be living under a great illusion, if they believed that territorial conquest would pay in the twentieth century. Given the interdependence of international finance, industry and commerce, Angell continued, a militarily victorious nation would, after the war, find its economic (and hence also its political) life in no less a shambles than the defeated opponent. In short, militarism and expansionism, at least according to Angell, no longer offered any benefits. In fact, it might even work more to the advantage of the vanquished than to that of the victor.

Apart from the range of historical data which were marshalled in support of this argument, the book is striking for its undiluted belief in the Idea of Progress. Later in his life, even Spencer became pessimistic about the notion that this Idea was advancing inexorably. Now, only four years before the outbreak of the First World War and four years after Hintze's forecasts, Angell came along to postulate that even in Germany, which many contemporaries saw as the epitome of Prussian militarism, the cooperative principle of industrialism was making progress against the 'parasitic' soldiers. And to underline his point, Angell also provided a kind of league table of nations which was supposed to chart the 'progression away from militancy' and which resulted in the following ranking order:[33]

> Arabia and Morocco,
> Turkish territory as a whole,
> The more unruly Balkan States. Montenegro,
> Russia,
> Spain, Italy, Austria,
> France,
> Germany,
> Scandinavia, Holland, Belgium,
> England.

After this table, can there still be any doubt about the developmental model which Angell, the writer in a typical liberal tradition, had in mind? To be sure, he was not a pacifist and his book is more concerned with national self-interest and the appeal to it than with international morality. 'Force', he wrote, 'will rule the world in the future as in the past, but it will be the force of hard work and superior brain, not the force of cannon and *Dreadnoughts*.[34] Society was changing under the impact of industrialism and with it human nature. Yet it was precisely at this point that Angell's optimism in effect appears to be a pre-1914 Liberal's whistling in the dark. He certainly gives a lot of space to what he calls 'the militarist case' before endeavouring to refute it.[35] In his attempt to undermine the argument of those who believed in the unchangeability of human nature, he presents an anthropogenesis which evolved from 'cannibalism' and slavery through various stages to, finally, industrial cooperation — at least in the West. How, he asked, can 'militarist writers' urge 'that non-military industrialism, which, with all its shortcomings, has on the Western Continent given us Canada and the United States, makes for decadence and degeneration, while militarism and the qualities and instincts that go with it have given us Venezuela and San Domingo?[36] On the contrary, if anything, industrial development would save those Latin American countries, with the 'one condition of their advance' being 'that they shall give up the stupid and sordid gold-braid militarism and turn to honest work'.

Enough has been said about Angell's *Great Illusion* to enable us to place it within a tradition of Anglo-Saxon thought on the subject of militarism and its supposedly inevitable decline. It was a tradition which, looking back, took a touchingly idealistic and naive view of the inherently peaceful nature of capitalist industrialism.

It was also a view of capitalism over which a fundamental disagreement developed between the liberal critics of militarism on the one hand, and the socialists, on the other. As the German Social Democrat Karl Liebknecht put it in 1906, militarism was 'typical of and essential to all class societies among which the capitalist one is merely the last'.[37] In other words, where Spencer had associated militarism with preindustrial regimes and believed that it would disappear once liberal capitalism was fully developed, the Marxists regarded all presocialist societies as militaristic. Militarism would disappear only after the advent of a communist system. Although this argument remained axiomatic to the discussion, it did not immediately result in a more coherent analysis by Marxist writers on the subject of militarism. To some extent this was due to the fact that Marx and Engels had accorded the concept of militarism rather a minor place in their interpretation of human history and were certainly never very systematic about defining it.

Perhaps an even more important reason for their neglect is to be found in their attitude towards force and war as historical phenomena. They were, after all, revolutionaries, not pacifists, even if their theory of revolutionary violence never evolved beyond its embryonic stages.[38] Furthermore they were concerned to show, in line with their 'materialist' conception of human history, that force was not endemic in human nature, as the Social Darwinists maintained, but derived from the political economy. This at least was the point over which Engels had his disagreement with Eugen Dühring,[39] and this is also what he expounded later in his pamphlet on the 'Role of Force in History'.[40] In his *Anti-Dühring* he wrote that 'force is not a simple act of will, but requires very concrete preconditions in order to make its application possible. Above all [it requires] instruments among which the more perfect ones will vanquish the less perfect'.[41] He added that these instruments 'must be produced, which implies at the same time that the producer of the more perfect instruments of violence, *vulgo* arms, will defeat the producer of less perfect ones'. In short, 'the victory of force rests upon the production of arms which in turn rests on production as such, i.e. on "economic power". . . .' To illustrate the functionality of force, Engels referred to the example of the master-slave relationship between Robinson Crusoe and Friday in Daniel Defoe's novel. What appears to be the use of force by one individual against another, so Engels argued, can in reality be reduced to a socio-economic relationship.

However, there was also an immediate political purpose behind Engel's preoccupation with the problem of force. His 'functionalist' interpretation of violence and, in its extreme form, of war was also designed, especially in his later work, to counter the hypothesis that arms races were a 'natural' state of affairs with an automaticity of their own. The Marxists saw arms races, on the contrary, as an outgrowth of a particular political economy. As Wilhelm Liebknecht, one of the founders of the German Social Democratic Party (SPD) put it in January 1882, such competitions encapsulated the 'whole essence of militarism'.[42] After the turn of the century, his son Karl emerged as on of the best-known spokesmen in the SPD on the subject of militarism. For him 'the history of militarism was identical with the history of political, social, economic and, in the most general sense, cultural tensions between states and nations and with the history of class struggles inside the individual states and national entities'.[43] To this extent there was nothing that was specific to 'capitalist militarism'. Nevertheless, by studying it as a special brand of militarism it was possible, Liebknecht continued, to 'lay bare the deepest, most hidden roots of capitalism'.

With this objective in mind, he then proceeded to examine the role of armies as instruments of capitalist class oppression and civil war during the phase of heightened class tension. He had studied the policies of the Prussian Army in Wilhelmine Germany and had found plenty of evidence to illustrate the maltreatment and disciplining of recruits, the spread of militarist ideas in society and the impact of military considerations on political decision-making.[44] The other half of his analysis was concerned with military power as an instrument of external war. This, he argued, was the other traditional function of armies whose foreign role had recently become supplemented by two further 'offshoots of capitalism in the military field': 'naval militarism' and 'colonial militarism'. In particular the latter was in Liebknecht's view largely responsible for cementing capitalist domination of overseas colonies by the most ruthless means of repression and destruction. German behaviour in South West Africa which greatly agitated public opinion at the time was to him merely one case in point.[45] Although Liebknecht spent some time discussing the effect of this 'external militarism', he did not embed it in a more general analysis of the dynamics of the capitalist system after the turn of the century. It is obvious that he was much more interested in the effect of militarism on the domestic situation and the culture of Wilhelmine society.

His priorities were also reflected in the avowed political purpose of his anti-militarist writings: the 'gradual organic subversion and attrition of the militarist spirit'. Although a professing Marxist, he is therefore not all that far apart from Quidde and other left-liberal critics of militarism. Liebknecht, it is true, was never one of the leading theoreticians of pre-1914 Social Democracy; but what in this case appears to have prevented him from arriving at a clear-cut theoretical position on the function and character of 'capitalist militarism' was that he used Prussia-Germany of all countries as his 'paradigm'. The trouble was that Wilhelmine Germany was not the fully developed capitalist-industrial society he assumed it to be. It was perhaps typical of Liebknecht's somewhat imprecise notion of militarism that he polemicized against Eduard Bernstein's view that the militaristic institutions of the day were a legacy of the feudal-monarchical period,[46] while happily assuming the Prusso-German monarchy to be the epitome of a capitalist militarism.

Rosa Luxemburg was noticeably more clear-headed than Liebknecht when she moved into this particular province of Marxist theory. At the beginning of 1899 she had been engaged in a dispute with the 'revisionist' Max Schippel in the pages of *Leipziger Volkszeitung*.[47] On

ALBRIGHT COLLEGE LIBRARY 207978

this occasion she stressed the economic function of modern militarism within a capitalist system which was showing a marked tendency towards concentration. From a social and political point of view, she added, militarism was the 'strongest pillar of [capitalist] class rule'; from an economic vantage-point, it was the 'most profitable and irreplaceable area of investment'. This idea which linked militarism with Marxist theories of imperialism reappears in an expanded and more refined version in her book *The Accumulation of Capital*, published in 1913.[48]

This book analysed 'militarism as a province of accumulation' during the various phases of the evolution of capitalism. It played, she wrote, 'a decisive part in the first stages of European capitalism, in the period of the so-called "primitive accumulation", as a means of conquering the New World and the spice-producing countries of India'. Subsequently militarism became employed in the acquisition of colonies 'to destroy the social organizations of primitive societies so that their means of production may be appropriated, forcibly to introduce commodity trade in countries where the social structure had been unfavourable to it and to turn the natives into a proletariat by com-pelling them to work for wages in the colonies'.

She also saw it as being 'responsible for the creation and expansion of spheres of interest for European capital in non-European regions, for extorting railway concessions in backward countries and for en-forcing the claims of European capital as international lender'. However important militarism may have been in these respects, another function was that it had become 'a pre-eminent means for the realisation of surplus value'. This, she continued, had occurred in two ways. Firstly, militarism had made 'a larger portion of surplus value available for capitalisation' because the maintenance of the repressive instru-ments of the capitalist state was largely paid for out of the wage packets of the workers by indirect taxation on food, drink etc., including the effect of protective tariffs. It was a simple calculation. For 'if the workers did not pay for the greater part of the state officials' upkeep, the capitalists themselves would have to bear the entire cost of it'. This would have meant that 'a corresponding portion of their surplus value would have to be assigned directly to keeping the organs of their class-rule, either at the expense of production which would have to be curtailed accordingly or, which is more probable, it would come from the surplus value intended for their consumption'.

Secondly, militarism created new opportunities for highly profitable investment 'when the monies concentrated in the exchequer by taxation are used for the production of armaments'. What is more: militarism enhanced economic concentration. For what was hitherto 'the multitude of individual and insignificant demands for a whole range of commodities', was being replaced by a 'comprehensive and homogeneous demand of the state'. Yet, 'the satisfaction of this demand presupposes a big industry of the highest order' operating under 'the most favourable conditions for the production of surplus value and for accumulation'. Thus, thanks to 'government contracts for army supplies the scattered purchasing power of the consumers is concentrated in large quantities and, free of the vagaries and subjective fluctuations of personal consumption, it achieves an almost automatic regularity and rhythmic growth'. However, the greatest advantage of armaments production was, Luxemburg believed, that it was capable of limitless expansion. While 'all other attempts to expand markets and set up operational bases for capital largely depend on historial, social and political factors beyond the control of capital,. . . production for militarism represents a province whose regular and progressive expansion seems primarily determined by capital itself'.

How would this controlling position be achieved? Through malleable representative assemblies and a capitalist-dominated press 'whose function [it] is to mould so called "public opinion"'. In the final analysis, Luxemburg's theory of militarism therefore aimed at explaining two developments: 'Capital increasingly employs militarism for implementing a foreign and colonial policy to get hold of the means of production and labour power of non-capitalist countries and societies'. But she also saw militarism evolving in the metropolitan countries as a way of diverting 'purchasing power away from the non-capitalist strata'. Thus, 'by robbing the one of their productive forces and by depressing the other's standard of living', the accumulation of capital and the evolution of capitalism would continue until, of course, and true to Marx's own teachings, the conditions thus created by the system 'become conditions for the decline of capitalism': 'The more ruthlessly capital sets about the destruction of non-capitalist strata at home and in the outside world, the more it lowers the standard of living for the workers as a whole, the greater also is the change in the day-to-day history of capital. It becomes a string of political and social disasters and convulsions and under these conditions, punctuated by periodical catastrophes and crises, accumulation can go on no longer.' It was only consistent with Luxemburg's own 'activist' theory of revolution that she did not conclude her analysis without having asserted that 'even before this natural economic impasse of capital's own creating is properly reached it becomes a necessity for the international working class to revolt against the rule of capital'.

The Accumulation of Capital is remarkable for the way in which it tried to combine a notion of 'capitalist militarism' with a theory of imperialism. While some key aspects of that latter theory may be flawed, Luxemburg was nevertheless among the first Marxist analysts who focused upon the function of armaments in the evolution of the industrial system. To her, arms races and wars of imperialist expansion were crucial areas which demonstrated the developing contradictions within capitalism. Of course, when she wrote her book, the arms race between the major European blocs was in full swing and there was a widespread feeling that a world war was not too far off. Yet when that war finally broke out in 1914, it and above all the concomitant collapse of working-class solidarity came as a shock to many Marxists. There were thus plenty of problems requiring explanation. Nikolai Bukharin was among the first to try to provide one. Taking Rudolf Hilferding's concept of *Finance Capital*[49] as his starting point, he postulated that

> Capitalist society is unthinkable without armaments, as it is unthinkable without wars. And just as it is true that not low prices cause competition but, on the contrary, competition causes low prices, it is equally true that not the existence of arms is the prime cause and the moving force in wars (although wars are obviously impossible without arms) but, on the contrary, the inevitableness of economic conflicts conditions the existence of arms. This is why in our times, when economic conflicts have reached an unusual degree of intensity, we are witnessing a mad orgy of armaments. Thus the rule of finance capital implies both imperialism and militarism. In this sense militarism is no less a typical historic phenomenon than finance capital itself.[50]

Although Bukharin's writings, together with Hobson's and Hilferding's, exerted an influence on the formulation of Lenin's famous theory of imperialism as 'the highest stage of capitalism',[51] there is little in Lenin's work that goes beyond prewar Marxist notions of the character of militarism. In an article which he published in 1908 he, too, merely emphasized the internal as well as external function of military power in capitalist countries.[52] And, of course, the advent of communism was for him the great dividing line beyond which militarism would become extinct.

The problem with most Marxist writings on the subject was that authors were too preoccupied with analysing the role and function of the military within the system in which they lived and whose manifest structural changes in the early decades of this century called for an elaboration, if not modification, of the original Marxian model. In so far as a socialist military programme and vision of the future role of armies was formulated at all, it hardly went beyond the simple slogan: 'Suppression of permanent armies, general arming of the people'.[53] The historian R.D. Challener is therefore quite right in arguing that 'socialist military thinking remained essentially negative throughout the nineteenth century'.[54] The most important exception to this rule is, of course, the work of the French socialist leader Jean Jaurès. Although he was influenced in his writings by Engels as well as his observations of the French and Swiss experience, it was he who tried to develop a coherent programme which he published in his famous book *L'armée nouvelle*.[55] In essence, it contained a concept of military organization which abolished not only the distinction between the army of the line and the reserve, but also between militia-men and citizens. Consequently, Jaurès proposed the dissolution of professional armies which he perceived to be instruments of aggression, to be replaced by citizens' armies which, he believed, could be used in defensive wars only. In this way, he more or less successfully gave some substance to pre-1914 socialist thought on the question of future military organization. His ideas on the role of armies under the existing capitalist system, on the other hand, did not move outside the mainstream of Marxist theory on this subject.

Looking back on the first fifty years of the debate on militarism, a number of significant developments have been identified. From the beginning, militarism was seen not just as a problem of military influence in politics and society, but also came to be placed by most authors into the framework of a developmental model of modern society. The question was not merely, when and under what circumstances militarism could be seen to exist, but also when and under what circumstances it would disappear. And it was over this latter problem that a deep rift opened up in the pre-1914 period between the Liberals and the Marxists. The First World War then merely exacerbated these differences of opinion although the actual experience of total war also knocked several holes into the arguments which the two sides had been presenting.

The main reason for the partial undermining of older positions appears to have been that neither the Liberals nor the Marxists had fully anticipated the impact of modern warfare upon the material life and the psychology of the participating nations. Of course, there were a number of writers who had advanced prophesies of future war and who had warned of a clash between the mass armies of the industrial nations.[56] Among these works, the six-volume study by the Polish-Russian banker and historian Jan Bloch, published in 1898, was perhaps the most exhaustive examination of the dangers of war.[57] But its predictions were, as far as can be seen, barely incorporated into the debate on militarism, largely it seems because Bloch was most concerned with technological warfare as such. However, perceptions of militarism changed after Europe had been exposed to the experience of total war and the next chapter will deal with this debate.

Notes

1   A. Roserot, ed., *Mme de Chastenay, Mémoires, 1717-1815*, Vol. 2, 2nd ed., Paris 1897, p.201, cited in W. Conze's contribution to O. Brunner et. al., eds., *Lexikon Geschichtlicher Grundbegriffe*, Vol. 4, Stuttgart 1978, p.21. On the difficulty of dating this entry precisely see ibid., note 104.
2   P.J. Proudhon, 'La Guerre et la Paix' in: P.J. Proudhon, *Oeuvres Complètes*, Paris 1868.
3   Cited in E. Assmuss, *Die publizistische Diskussion um den Militarismus unter besonderer Berücksichtigung der Geschichte des Begriffes in Deutschland und seiner Beziehung zu den politischen Ideen zwischen 1850 und 1950*, PhD. dissertation, University of Erlangen, 1951, p.36.
4   Cited in M. Geyer's contribution to O. Brunner et al., eds., *Lexikon Geschichtlicher Grundbegriffe*, p.25.
5   E. Assmuss, *Die publizistische Diskussion*, p.31.
6   For the German orientalist Hugo Winckler, Assyria was a militaristic state. The British historian Arnold Toynbee considered Sparta to be the paradigm of militarism. See A. Toynbee, *War and Civilisation*, London 1951, pp.26ff. More recently, the Cambridge historian Moses Finley has cast some doubt upon Toynbee's view when he found that 'militarism in Sparta was in a low key'. See M.I. Finley, 'Sparta' in: J.P. Vernant, ed., *Problèmes de la Guerre en Grèce Ancienne*, Paris 1968, p.154. See also A. Vagts, *History of Militarism*, pp. 12f.
7   On this question see below, pp. 14f.
8   H. Herzfeld, 'Der Militarismus als Problem der neueren deutschen Geschichte' (1946), reprinted in: V.R. Berghahn, ed., *Militarismus*, p.110. The year 1660 might be considered a more crucial turning point.
9   Declaration of Independence, reprinted in: R. Hofstadter et al., eds., *The American Republic*, Vol. 1, Englewood Cliffs 1959, p.685.
10 For a fuller discussion see W. Conze's contribution to O. Brunner et al., eds., *Lexikon Geschichtlicher Grundbegriffe*, pp.8ff., also for the following.
11 A. Vagts, *A History of Militarism*, p.15.
12 See, e.g., F. E. Manuel, *The New World of Henri Saint-Simon*, Cambridge (Mass.) 1956; G. Ionescu, ed., *The Political Thought of Saint-Simon*, Oxford 1976; R. Fletcher, ed., *The Crisis of Industrial Civilisation*, London 1974; K. Taylor, ed., *Henri Saint-Simon*, London 1975, pp.194-95.
13 See, e.g., W. Schulz-Bodmer, *Die Rettung der Gesellschaft aus den Gefahren der Militärherrschaft*, Leipzig 1859. His work is discussed in M. Geyer's contribution to O. Brunner et al., eds., *Lexikon Historischer Grundbegriffe*, pp.22ff.
14 G.M. Pachtler, *Der europäische Militarismus*, Amberg 1875.
15 P. Wasserburg, *Gedankenspäne über den Militarismus*, Mainz 1874, quoted in: E. Assmuss, *Die publizistische Diskussion*, p.43.

16 H. Spencer, *The Principles of Sociology,* Vol. II/2, New York-London 1886, pp.568-602, also for the following quotations.

17 Ibid., p.603-642, also for the following quotations.

18 On Spencer's general system of beliefs, see D. Wiltshire, *The Social and Political Thought of Herbert Spencer,* Oxford 1978.

19 The original version of Hintze's essay on 'Staatsverfassung und Heeresverfassung' was a lecture sponsored by the Gehe-Stiftung at Dresden and delivered on 17 February 1906. A translation is now available in: F. Gilbert, ed., *The Historical Essays of Otto Hintze,* New York 1975, pp.180-215. The following quotations are taken from this translation.

20 See, e.g., his essays, ibid., pp. 216ff.

21 N.N., *Der Militarismus im heutigen deutschen Reich,* Stuttgart 1893.

22 Ibid., p.27.

23 Ibid., p.34.

24 For an interesting study of the pre-1914 Peace Movement in Germany see R. Chickering, *Imperial Germany and a World Without War,* Princeton 1975. The value of this study lies in the fact that it uses the relative unpopularity of the German Peace Movement as a mirror in which to reflect the strength of militarism in Wilhelmine society.

25 A well-known representative of this school of thought was Friedrich Naumann. See his essay 'Demokratie und Kaisertum' in: F. Naumann, *Werke,* Vol. 2, Cologne 1964.

26 On Bleibtreu see M. Geyer's contribution to O. Brunner et al., eds., *Lexikon Historischer Grundbegriffe,* p.33. However, in the last years before the First World War such views were no longer unusual and a 'cult of violence' had gained considerable popularity not merely in Germany, but also in other European countries. See, e.g., E. Nolte, *The Three Faces of Fascism,* New York 1969; C. Tisdall and A. Bozolla, *Futurism,* London 1977; G. Eley, *Reshaping the German Right,* New Haven 1980.

27 J.D. Miller, 'Militarism or Manhood?' *Arena* (1900), pp.379-92; reprinted in R.F. Weighley, ed., *The American Military,* Reading (Mass.) 1966, pp.85-92. The following quotations are taken from Weigley's edition.

28 See, especially, J.A. Schumpeter's famous essay 'Zur Soziologie der Imperialismen' (1919), transl. in J.A. Schumpeter, *Imperialism,* Oxford 1951.

29 J.A. Hobson, *Imperialism. A Study,* London 1902.

30 G. Ferrero, *Il Militarismo,* Milano 1898, English transl. London 1902. Quotations taken from the English version.

31 N. Angell, *Europe's Optical Illusion, London 1909.*

32 See also A.J.A. Morris, *Radicalism Against War, 1906-1914,* London 1972, pp.20ff. All quotations from Angell's book are taken from the 3rd ed., publ. in 1911.

33 N. Angell, *The Great Illusion,* p.191.

34 Ibid., p.108.

35 Ibid., pp.143ff.

36 Ibid., p.187.

37 K. Liebknecht, 'Militarismus und Antimilitarismus unter besonderer Berücksichtigung der internationalen Jugendbewegung', reprinted in V.R. Berghahn, ed., *Militarismus,* p.89.

38 For a general discussion see W. Wette, *Kriegstheorien deutscher Sozialisten,* Stuttgart 1971.

39   F. Engels, 'Herrn Eugen Dührings Umwälzung der Wissenschaft' in *Marx-Engels-Werke*, Vol. 20, Berlin 1960, pp.147ff.

40   Ibid., Vol. 21, pp.405ff.

41   Ibid., Vol. 20, p.148.

42   Quoted in M. Geyer's contribution to O. Brunner et al., eds., *Lexikon Historischer Grundbegriffe*, p.35.

43   K. Liebknecht, 'Militarismus und Antimilitarismus', reprinted in V.R. Berghahn, ed., *Militarismus*, p.86

44   Much of this material was later collected by R. Höhn, *Sozialismus und Heer*, Bad Homburg 1959, and R. Höhn, *Die Armee als Erziehungsschule der Nation*, Bad Harzburg 1963.

45   On this subject see H. Bley, *Kolonialherrschaft und Sozialstruktur in Deutsch-Südwestafrika, 1894-1914*, Hamburg 1968.

46   E. Bernstein in *La Vie Socialiste*, 5.6.1905.

47   R. Luxemburg, *'Miliz und Militarismus' Leipziger Volkszeitung, 20-22*, and 25.2.1899, reprinted in R. Luxemburg, *Gesammelte Werke*, Vol. I/1, Berlin 1970, pp.446-66.

48   R. Luxemburg, *Die Akkumulation des Kapitals*, Berlin 1913, English transl. London 1951. The following quotations are taken from this translation.

49   R. Hilferding, *Finanzkapital. Eine Studie über die jüngste Entwicklung des Kapitalismus*, Vienna 1910.

50   N.I. Bukharin, *Imperialism and World Economy*, New York 1966, p.127. The study was written in 1915 and published in Russian in 1917.

51   V.I. Lenin, *Imperialism, the Highest Stage of Capitalism* (1917), Moscow 1966.

52   V.I. Lenin, 'Der streitbare Militarismus und die antimilitaristische Taktik der Sozialdemokratie' in V.I. Lenin, *Werke*, Vol. 15, Berlin 1962, pp.186-96. First published in *Proletarii*, 23.7. (5.8.) 1908.

53   R.D. Challener, *The French Theory of the Nation in Arms, 1866-1939*, New York 1965, p.68.

54   Ibid., p.69.

55   J. Jaurès, *L'armée nouvelle*, Paris 1915.

56   I.S. Clark, *Voices Prophesying War*, Oxford 1966.

57   J. Bloch, [*The War of the Future in Its Technical, Economic and Political Relations*], 6 vols., St. Petersburg 1898, with an abridged English translation — *Is War Now Impossible?*, London 1899. See also T.H.E. Travers, 'Technology, Tactics and Morale: Jean de Bloch, the Boer War and Military Theory, 1900-1914'. *Journal of Modern History* 51 (1979), pp.264-86.

II   The Impact of Two Total Wars

While the Marxists had arrived at a broad consensus before and during the First World War regarding the basic nature of militarism, the non-Marxist debate continued inconclusively after 1914 and developed a curious twist. In the West, the traditional arguments of the Liberals were advanced with renewed vigour. French, British and American soldiers marched to the front in defence of civilian parliamentary government against the Prussian jackboot. Allied propaganda left little doubt that the struggle against German militarism was at the same time a struggle against destructive forces generated by the backward and inferior social and political systems of the Dual Alliance. It was the already familiar arsenal of arguments that was employed in the West.

A similarly powerful ideology emerged in Germany, but with the value judgments reversed. To paraphrase the title of Werner Sombart's well-known study,[1]* the War was seen as a struggle by the heroic and superior *Kultur* of the Germanic nations against the petty commercialism and base materialism of Anglo-Saxon *Zivilisation*: heroes vs. traders. Suddenly Germany's fate appeared to hinge on the quality of her military institutions. Even those intellectuals and academics who had previously been mildly critical of the position of the Army in German politics and society were now prepared to regard it as an integral part of German culture about whose superior quality there was no doubt. When Ernst Troeltsch, an eminent theologian, lectured on the topic of 'Our People's Army' in November 1914, militarism had a positive ring to his ear. It implied

> that Germany, because of her continental position, with her very poor natural frontiers and as a latecomer among the European nations which is threatened from all sides, must bear the burden of heavy armaments and perfect these armaments at all cost. . . . Militarism means furthermore that the military organization rubs off to a certain extent on our entire civilian life. . . . Militarism

*The notes for this chapter begin on page 47.

finally implies that we do not just cherish and uphold our Army because we are impelled by rational calculations, but also because we felt an irresistible compulsion within our hearts to love it.[2]

Like Troeltsch, most other academics felt called upon to extol the virtues of militarism.[3] In 1915, 1347 of them signed an appeal in defence of the monarchy's policies and institutions. A year later, the economist Goetz Briefs published an article on 'State, Political Liberty and Militarism in Germany' which appeared in a collection of essays designed to refute a French book on the suject of *La Guerre Allemande et le Catholicisme*.[4] The cultural and political theme became a central issue in the ideological war. Hintze's volume on *Deutschland und der Weltkrieg*[5] contained, *inter alia*, an essay by the historian Friedrich Meinecke who, writing from a Protestant perspective, produced his own idealized picture of 'Culture, Politics and Militarism'. At about the same time, Nahum Goldmann, later the President of the World Jewish Congress, published a booklet on the *Geist des Militarismus*[6] in which he argued that the military spirit had also come to dominate the non-military aspects of Germany's life.[7] The 'principles on which the Army is built have also become the principles of German national life in general, of the German spirit and of German *Kultur*. The fact that the nation had been put into a uniform was seen by him as the assertion of the democratic principle. Militarism had assumed the importance of a basic cultural value.

All these writings were obviously not particularly helpful to an understanding of our problem, except that they tell us a good deal about the state of German society and, more generally, about the impact of the First World War on the participant countries. And once it was over, the search for what it had meant intensified. The economic and political repercussions, it is true, were most visible and immediate, and historians have therefore tended to pay less attention to another major effect: the psychological one. Compared with how the majority of the population reacted to the War in the Anglo-Saxon countries, the development in Central Europe once more took a different turn. In the West, the experience of trench warfare and massive bloodshed reinforced pacifist currents without, however, adding genuinely new arguments to the anti-militarist armoury.[8] They reappeared in different guises in Britain during the interwar debate on conscription or in the discussions on disarmament in the League of Nations.[9] In a different way they may also be discerned in the military clauses of the Versailles Treaty which reduced Germany's military power to a 100,000-man army and disbanded the General Staff, in the eyes of many Anglo-Saxons the citadel of Prussian militarism. Although similar anti-militarist currents arose in Germany, the balance of forces was different here. The 1920s witnessed the rise of strong militaristic movements and organizations which left a deep imprint upon Weimar politics.[10]

The roots of this postwar militarism are to be found not only in the intensive mobilization of the population under the banner of the above-mentioned 'positive' militarism of the period 1914-18, but also in the defeat which broad sections of the nation flatly refused to accept. They continued to believe in the essential superiority of the German type of political and social organization and escaped into a world of myths and legends. In their view there was nothing fundamentally wrong with German culture. What had been lacking was the determination and 'will-power' necessary to generate and sustain a unified national effort. It is worthwhile looking briefly at the arguments of those who openly and proudly called themselves 'militarists' and who joined the paramilitary associations of the Weimar period in their hundreds of thousands.

The Canadian historian Warren E. Williams has studied the outward trappings of what he called the 'paramilitarism' of the interwar period.[11] No doubt these manifestations represented a very interesting and telling aspect of the phenomenon of militarism: exact copies of the German Army with the same rigid command structures and hierarchies, the same military terminology and language, and all the paraphernalia. They held parades and marches at local level, organized field exercises in remote forests beyond the reach of the Inter-Allied Military Control Commission and treated themselves to a major annual rally in some politically sensitive city during which family-fathers and 'respectable' middle-aged gentlemen put up with the inconveniences of a Boy Scout existence. They devotedly slept in tents and queued up to have their meals dished out to them by field kitchens.[12] It was an experience which had a great emotional significance for them.

Nevertheless, the ideas behind these movements are conceivably more important than these external aspects of 'paramilitarism'. One main dividing line which can be discerned is that between a nostalgic and a 'modern' militarism. Thus a number of organizations cherished a purely backward-looking view of politics and society. To them everything that the Prussian Army of the pre-1914 period had stood for and believed in was good and worth preserving. On the other hand, there were quite a few associations or members within a particular organization who maintained that the old world of Wilhelmine militarism has collapsed under the impact of total war. The 'State of the Front

Soldiers', i.e. the state of those who had returned from the battle fields with the lessons of the First World War in their hearts, was to be organized along different lines.[13] The war, they said, had led to the establishment of a community of the trenches in which class differences had ceased to count and to exist. The task was now to secure the continuation of the *Schützengrabengemeinschaft* in peacetime. It was therefore most unfortunate that the largest single section of the population, the working class, had 'dropped out' of this community at the end of the war. The big question which this group of 'modern' militarists asked themselves (among whom the novelist Ernst Jünger became the most prominent figure) was how it might be possible to overcome the alienation of the workers from the idea of the *Frontsoldatenstaat*. Jünger did not believe that the working class could be persuaded to return to the national fold by means of a policy of superficial economic concessions, as advocated by certain right-wing circles at the time. Social appeasement was not what he had in mind. His vision of the Front Soldiers' State, which explicitly included the workers, was much more daring and, for the purposes of our analysis, also much more significant.

The solution he envisaged was first published in an essay entitled *The Total Mobilization*[14] and in 1932 in his book *The Worker*[15] which made a tremendous impact at a crucial moment in German history. In fact, it is not too far-fetched to say that it was the most important book published in Germany at a time when the National Socialists were making their bid for power. To understand Jünger's preoccupation with the worker, his ideas must be seen not only in a military context, but also within the framework of what he considered to be the other decisive force of the modern period, i.e. industrialization. His twentieth-century formula for the organization of an ideal society tried to take account of both a militarized nationalism and the appearance of modern industrial technology.

Jünger would perhaps never have found a solution to the political problems of his time, as he perceived them, had it not been for the experience of total war which he went through as a young man. War was the hub of his system of ideas around which everything else revolved. And in the phenomenon of war he had also discovered a common bond which he believed existed between the soldier and the industrial worker. It consisted, he argued, in their attitude towards technology. To Jünger modern life appeared as a gigantic work process which stretched over times of war as well as of peace. The warrior was engaged in the most dangerous type of work, yet work it was nonetheless. The *Materialschlacht* whether in the factory or on the battle-field was the most concrete expression of the twentieth century. Thus the man of the trenches is seen by Jünger as the representative of a new race who is a kin of the industrial worker and who uses his tools with the same skill as the man in the factory; the differences being that the soldier's work is of a lethal nature. The implication was that to Jünger the experience of war was no longer just a nationalistic delirium. It was a work process in which a worker-soldier wielded his tools with cold-blooded precision. He operated a factory of death.

War, so Jünger believed, is not only a passionate, but also a cut and dried business, 'a hammering march which in one's mind gives rise to images of huge industrial districts, armies of machines, work battalions and calculating men of power'.[16] In war, and in war alone, modern technology and the strength of the human spirit became combined in a most powerful and new formula. The productive forces locked up in it led Jünger to

> see a new leading race emerging in ancient Europe, a fearless and fabulous race which does not shy away from the sight of blood, which is reckless and used to suffering as well as perpetrating terrible things and which aims for the highest achievement. I see a race which builds machines and defies them, a race to which machines are organs of power rather than dead scraps of iron, machines which will be commanded with a cool mind and a passionate heart. This will give a new face to the world.

In other words, it was the coming of the Age of Steel that was being predicted here. It would be nationalistic as well as martial, making use of all the means of modern technology and with the worker-soldier as a sort of superman at the controls.

Inevitably, Jünger's prophesy of the promised land was at the same time a prognosis of doom. Again it had been during the First World War that he had seen 'in lethally sparkling mirrors the collapse of an age which was hopelessly lost'. On one level, this was the age of Western rationalism and liberalism. But Jünger's strong anti-Western-ism was based on something more than mere resentment stemming from the humiliation of 1918 and the Versailles settlement. The citizen of the Occident represented in Jünger's world of ideas a type of man who was incapable of making sacrifices. He was a man who would talk about his rights rather than his duties; he was a man who needed peace to find fulfilment. The contrast could also be put into *'national'* terminology. To Jünger, the man whose tools consisted of a cheque-book and who would never stop thinking of his business was Anglo-Saxon by definition. The man whose equipment were the steel-helmet

and the machine-gun, on the other hand, was quintessentially German.
Hence Jünger's total rejection of Anglo-Saxon ways of life and institutions; hence also his hatred of the Weimar Republic which he
thought to be a mere creature of the Western Allies. It was logical
therefore that this Republic had to be destroyed before the State of the
Front Soldiers could be built, and Jünger certainly came to approve of
any means which helped to undermine the Weimar system. To witness
the end of the bourgeois age, he once said, would be a great day for
him.

A complicating factor was that, as Jünger observed, bourgeois
values and attitudes prevailed not only in the West and among the
supporters of the Weimar Republic; they could also be discovered
guiding the actions of former front soldiers who were marching in the
endless columns of organized militarism. It was from their particular
'revolutionary' vantage-point that the young intellectuals around
Jünger began to pour scorn over all proclivities to return to prewar
ways of life. By comparison with the New Nationalism of the interwar
period, Wilhelmine militarism was regarded as old-fashioned and
hollow. It represented

> the shapelessness with which the patriotic sentiment of the
> Imperial a yearning for revenge, in Germany it was the rattling of
> sabres, the drumming of tins, the throwing about of words. . . .
> School-boys learned to bang their fists against their cardboard-
> armoured chest when, on national holidays, they recited martial
> poems. Sedan Day meant good business for manufacturers of
> fire-crackers and Germany saw herself illuminated.[17]

Clearly, the new German Reich, shaped by ex-soldiers who
had transcended the atmosphere of the 'good old days', was not to be
compared with the Reich of Wilhelm II. The rejection of the backward-
looking tendencies of the older generation was accompanied by a
permanent appeal to end particularism and haggles over leadership
which were so typical of German veterans' associations in the era
of the Weimar Republic after World War I. More than once Jünger
launched a vigorous protest against shortsightedness and egotism. He
later added complaints about the deplorable dullness of the corps of
paramilitarist functionaries who exhausted themselves in the mindless
task of organizing. At times the bitterness which these realities
engendered among the younger generation found expression in sarcastic
comments such as the criticism which appeared in one journal in 1926.[18]
In dealing with the problems posed by the review of very large con-
tingents during the Düsseldorf Front Soldiers' Day the anonymous

author suggested that it might have been more practical to have had the members assembled in one double column. In this way the organizers would have obtained a line-up twelve miles long so that the review could have been completed by car or preferably by plane in a fraction of the actual time taken.

This story illustrates well the differences between the Prussian-style militarism and that of Jünger. The 'new militarists' did not wish to attract 'warriors who sleep in bourgeois bedrooms'. They wanted to build a heroic society upon the ruins of the old which had shown itself to be obsessed with status distinctions and lacking in soldierly virtues. In the end this message of the 'new militarism' proved so powerful that the leagues on the Left of the political spectrum likewise adopted elements of its ideology and style of operation.[19] 'Paramilitarism' became a phenomenon which pervaded virtually all aspects of German political life and made a strong impact also in some other countries. In view of this, it is not surprising that many contemporary analysts, when observing the style and the politics of the interwar *Wehrverbände*, should have found the psychological and psychopathological dimensions of interwar militarism most noteworthy.

One of them, Friedrich Sternthal, wrote in 1921 that it was 'not the existence of a large army with all its accessories' which was decisive for an understanding of the problem, but 'the subordination of all other aspects [of life] to the military one and the domination of civilian life by military ideas and values'.[20] Franz Carl Endres, the military affairs correspondent of the liberal *Frankfurter Zeitung*, finally even went so far as to define militarism as 'the state of mind of the non-military'.[21] A country, he wrote elsewhere, 'can have an extraordinarily strong army without being militaristic', just as there can be militarism in the absence of a strong army, as in Weimar Germany.[22] It was the all-pervasive 'spirit of the uniform' which was the key to the problem. Similar arguments were advanced in this period by pacifist writers such as Friedrich Wilhelm Foerster and Alfred Fried.

While most authors tended to see militarism as belonging to the realm of ideas and of attitudes towards social reality, it would be wrong to give the impression that its sociological dimension was now completely lost sight of. Endres's writings are a good case in point. Although he described militarism as a state of mind, he nevertheless entitled his article of 1927 'Sociological Structure and Related Ideologies among the Prewar German Officer Corps' and published it in *Archiv für Sozialwissenschaft und Sozialpolitik*. Foerster wrote on another occasion that 'militarism was the mode of Prussian society', even if he did not elaborate on how this society was structured.[23]

These analytical vacillations between militarism as an ideological and a sociological phenomenon also characterize the works of Eckart Kehr[24] and Heinz Fick.[25] Kehr in particular tied the concept to the existence of an officer corps upholding the ethos of a warrior caste and to the acceptance of this ethos as a higher form of human order by the civilian bourgeoisie. At the same time he proposed to analyse this acceptance 'closely in connection with the recent confrontation between the [emergent] capitalist society in Prussia and the rising industrial proletariat'. Fick was similarly concerned on the one hand with the spread of 'militarist thinking in German intellectual life and the specific morphology of this style of thinking';[26] on the other, he took great pains to stress the link between militarism and feudalism and argued that the social and political structures of East Elbia helped to provide the economic base of Prussian militarism. Moreover, he dealt with other social groups which were originally hostile to militarism and explained that, with the passage of time, the economic interests of the entrepreneur began to coincide with his support of militarism. Wilhelm Reich finally tried to bridge the gap between the psycho-pathology of militarism and the socio-economic structure by means of his theory of sexuality.[27] He believed he had discovered a link between an individual's physical bearing and the structure of the social order in which he lived. Dictatorial-militaristic systems, he maintained, which were committed to destroying independence of mind, reproduced themselves in the stiffly upright military gait of their subjects.

Then, in 1937/38, there appeared in New York and London a book by Alfred Vagts which represented one of the fullest and most important attempts to come to terms with the problem of militarism.[28] Vagts was a refugee from Nazism and belonged to a small group of historians around Kehr who had gone to the United States. His work is a general empirical treatment of the subject and hence very different from the approach taken in this study. Vagts starts with a discussion of the 'feudal warrior' of the Middle Ages and then traces the 'romance and realities of a profession', i.e. the military one, down to the twentieth century. While these chapters contain a great deal of historical material, they are preceded by a longer introduction on 'the idea of the nature of militarism' which may be taken to represent an attempt to pull the various threads of the non-Marxist debate together.

At a most general level, Vagts sees militarism as a 'tendency to extend dominion' and thus explicitly puts it side-by-side with the coeval concept of imperialism. The latter, he adds, 'looks primarily for more territory', while the former 'covets more men and more money'. Viewed from this perspective, militarism is, of course, a very ancient phenomenon which existed at different times in various parts of the world. Thus 'the ancient Assyrians afford the clearest demonstration of past imperialism and militarism'. Vagts then goes on to differentiate between that older type of militarism and a 'modern' one which possesses specific traits. The difference arises because modern armies 'are not so constantly engaged in combat as were the ancient armies'. As a result they tend to become 'narcissistic — they dream that they exist for themselves alone'. And an army which is constructed in such a way that 'it serves military men, not war, is militaristic' and 'so is everything in an army which is not preparation for fighting, but merely exists for diversion or to satisfy peacetime whims like the long-anachronistic cavalry today'.

It now becomes clear that Vagts is making a crucial distinction between an army which 'is maintained in a military way' and one that operates in a 'militaristic way'. The military way, he continues, 'is marked by a primary concentration of men and materials on winning specific objectives of power with the utmost efficiency; that is, with the least expenditure of blood and treasure. It is limited in scope, confined to one function and scientific in its essential qualities'. Militarism, by contrast, 'presents a vast array of customs, interests, prestige, actions and thought associated with armies and wars and yet transcending the true military purposes'. Moreover, 'its influence is unlimited in scope'. It can even 'permeate all society and become dominant over all industry and arts'. Whereas the military way displays a 'scientific character', militarism upholds 'the qualities of caste and cult, authority and belief'. Hence Vagts does not reject the existence of military apparatuses in principle. In fact he emphasizes that not even militarism is 'the opposite of pacifism'. For 'militarism is more, and sometimes less, than the love of war', whose true counterpart would be 'love of peace', i.e. pacifism. Instead militarism 'covers every system of thinking and valuing and every complex of feelings which rank military institutions and ways above the ways of civilian life, carrying military mentality and modes of action and decision into the civilian sphere'.

In the final analysis, Vagts therefore tries to blend the Central European preoccupation with militarism as a state of mind with Anglo-Saxon concerns of civilian control. The latter approach emerges most clearly at the end of the Introduction: where both civilians and the military have 'an informed and realistic conception of society's interests', frictions between them will be removed and the militarists 'could be subordinated to the military'. Where, on the other hand, 'civilian policies are constructed without regard to their military implications, with reckless disregard of war potentials and money is voted for military establishments blindly, without knowing. . . whether it is to be spent in a military or a militaristic manner, the maintenance of peace and of society itself' will be threatened. It is in this way that Vagts ultimately arrives at an explanation of militarism, the 'militarism of moods and opinions', that 'has been more clearly in evidence in Germany than elsewhere, except in Japan, because there the soldier has been admired in peace-time and not, as in other lands, mostly in war. Even in peace, the German is inclined to acknowledge the primacy of the military and accept its absolute good regardless of its use in war, its victories or defeats.' Nevertheless, he adds, it would be misleading to confine the use of the concept to that country alone. Militarism is to be found elsewhere in the West, even if it is 'relatively modern' there.

In his search for the origins of this modern militarism, Vagts finally goes back to the Romantic period and the end of the eighteenth century. This was the time when 'the old rationalism of the Enlightenment which regarded the soldier as a drilled murderer was being submerged in resurgent emotionalism and the glory of "romance" was being spread over the drab realities of war and the commonplaces of the Industrial Revolution'. At the end of this process there emerged what Vagts calls 'mass militarism'. But — and here he made an explicit reference to the social base of militarism — it found no support among the middle-classes 'represented by English Utilitarians, Continental Liberals and American Rationalists of the constitutional period'. On the contrary, these groups were 'distrustful of militarism, fearing to lose the fruits of their emancipation by such backward yearning for times and institutions hostile to their own developing interests'. Rather it was made and propagated by 'the upper and the lower classes, the captivating and the captivated classes'. It was 'the former, the Tory or conservative forces', that 'strove to reerect what Edmund Burke called the state of the "knights and saints" and sought mass support through its Romantic appeals'. And according to Vagts, they did obtain this mass support. Thanks to the propaganda efforts of politicians and military historians, 'the cottagers were soon to "know no other history" than that of a glorious military past'.

Vagts finds this line particularly strongly developed in early nineteenth-century France. To him 'Thiers is among the first in that line of bourgeois-civilian writers given to the praise of militarism, whose hybrid figures haunted Carlyle, Treitschke, Theodore Roosevelt, Nietzsche, Barrès, Charles Maurras and Kipling. They all praised army institutions and army men, some for obedience and others for leadership, exulting, as in the case of Carlyle, over the "commander of men"'. These sentiments, he continued, fell on fertile soil 'among

those who had learned to feel the horrors and uncertainties of industrialization. While even those who fared comfortably sometimes
turned backward in nostalgic appreciation of the Middle Ages, millions
of workers and farmers, finding no great profit or enjoyment in their
new freedom, sought solace from their isolation in the growing life of
societies, clubs and party organizations'. As individuals, 'the nineteenth-
century masses' hated war, but as a collective they came to love it. It
may be, Vagts argued, that the attitude of the 'modern masses towards
militarism' was contradictory; yet this did not prevent its further
spread until it was ultimately taken up by Fascism and Communism.

It is at this point that Vagts's sociology of militarism is thrown into
sharp relief. He interprets it as a phenomenon of modern mass society
without attempting a sociological break-down of these 'masses'. Militarism has become an all-embracing problem and even the Salvation
Army is mentioned by him as one among a multitude of civilian
organizations of his time which attempts 'to get hold of military
instincts in the service of religious philanthropy'. By now, one may
assume, even the liberal middle-classes have been infected by these
instincts since 'military arrangements and discipline have become a
great pattern for individual employers or managers under industrialism'. Vagts's analysis had, of course, one serious drawback: with
everybody having become part of an amorphous mass worshipping
militarism, the question of the functionality of militarism which
so interested the early Marxists and which continued to preoccupy
Marxist analysts in the 1930s, faded and militarism itself had been
given rather a wide mantle. The term was hardly made more specific
when Vagts asserted furthermore that 'at the very bottom of the
civilian order the isolated individual wants to find himself in a
more congenial, less quarrelsome company than that provided by his
business employment or his relatives'. In modern society he tries to
'find this relief in the mass movements and processions in which the
equal step, the music of bands and mass chanting drown out, tem-
porarily, the dissensions of ordinary life'. It is 'by way of such illusions'
that 'militarization has overtaken a large section of the elements that
are known in the United States as "joiners" comprising not only
ex-soldiers, but marchers called by "knightly" names and bearing
"knightly" insignia, and the class warriors [!]'.

Enough has been said about Vagts's *History of Militarism* and the
conceptual framework underlying the book to pinpoint its strengths
and weaknesses. It was written, against the background of the Weimar
experience, in a tradition of Western liberalism in which the problem
of the civilian control of the military had always occupied a prominent

place. But this control had been slipping because the civilians, with the advent of mass politics, had themselves become militaristic. Vagts felt that it had become impossible in the twentieth century to specify who these 'masses' were. This does not prevent him from trying to analyse their state of mind, and in this respect he can be placed into a particular tradition of thought which gained a good deal of popularity among Republican critics of militarism in Weimar Germany. The fact that Vagts had grown up surrounded by that tradition may help to explain not merely his interest in militarism as a totalitarian phenomenon, but also his predominantly history-of-ideas approach. To this extent the book brought together the Western and the Central European non-Marxist critique in a comprehensive analysis. On the whole, it remained weak on the economy and sociology of militarism. Above all, however, it contained curiously little on the technological and bureaucratic aspects of the problem. In fact, Vagts deliberately excluded them from his study. For militarism, he wrote, does not exist

> when armies call for and make efficient, rational, up-to-date and, to a certain extent, human use of the materials and forces available to them; when they prepare themselves for war decided upon, not by themselves, but by the civilian powers of the state; . . . when they get ready for the true future war which is not "in the air", but which takes the form of an image deduced from the general economy of contemporary society and from the materials it produces as war materials.

It will be seen below that Vagts, in excluding these aspects, may have adopted too restrictive a definition. Certainly this restriction of his subject comes as a surprise when a self-styled militarist like Jünger has made so much of the industrial dimension in his own writings in the early 1930s. And there were other writers who had argued as early as 1915/16 that, mass mobilization apart, the First World War had added a new factor to the problem of militarism. Especially Goldmann, but also men like Walther Rathenau recognised the impact of the organizational revolution which that war had caused in the administrative and technological-industrial sphere. Goldmann was the first to speak of 'industrial soldiers' and to be struck by the bureaucratic dynamics of the war situation.[29] The German-American historian Michael Geyer has, in view of these clearly observable developments, rightly spoken of an 'Organized Militarism' which, he argues, came into existence at this time and side-by-side with 'Organized Capitalism'.[30] However, this was not a publicly visible militarism similar to that of the para-military leagues of the interwar period. It was a 'militarism' the existence of which had to be lifted from the archives of the German Army Ministry. Vagts may therefore be forgiven for not attaching the importance to technological change and bureaucratic tendencies which they deserve for an understanding of militarism in the twentieth century.

It is in this latter connection that Harold D. Lasswell's article of 1941 on 'The Garrison State and the Specialists on Violence' must be mentioned.[31] In one respect, Lasswell may be said to have continued along the path of Pachtler who had first expressed the fear that modern society might develop into a 'huge garrison'.[32] Writing some 65 years later, Lasswell proposed 'to consider the possibility that we are moving toward a world of "garrison states"'.[33] It would be a world 'in which the specialists on violence are the most powerful group in society'. Lasswell was the first to admit that he was not predicting 'something wholly new under the sun'. Spencer, for instance, had been concerned with a type of state based on force. But what Lasswell tried to envisage was 'the possible emergence of the military state under present technical conditions'. At least he could not think of any previous examples of a Spencerian 'military state combined with modern technology' and went on to postulate that 'the military men who dominate a modern technical society will be very different from the officers of history and tradition'. The Garrison State, to be sure, would not emerge overnight. There may be transitions in the form of 'the party propaganda state, where the dominant figure is the propagandist, and the party bureaucratic state, in which the organization men of the party make the vital decisions'. On the other hand, Lasswell was convinced that 'the trend of our time is away from the specialist on bargaining, who is the businessman, and toward the supremacy of the soldier'.

One major reason for this, apart from the increasing availability of improved technology, was that 'the socialization of danger' had become a 'permanent characteristic of modern violence' and had turned a particular nation into a 'unified technical enterprise'. This meant that 'those who direct the violence operations are compelled to consider the entire gamut of problems that arise in living together under modern conditions'. One inevitable consequence of this was, in Lasswell's view, that these 'specialists on violence are more preoccupied with the skills and attitudes judged characteristic of nonviolence'. They will 'include in their training a large degree of expertness in many of the skills that we have traditionally accepted as part of modern civilian management'. Ultimately they would therefore also operate more like managers of industrial enterprises although they would not function as independent decision-makers in a free market situation. The Garrison State, Lasswell continued, would be

highly centralized and bureaucratized; there would be definite hierarchies, albeit more complex than those to be found in a traditional
military command structure. This would raise the problem of control.
For example, 'there is so much outspoken resistance to bureaucratism
in modern civilization that we may expect this attitude to carry over to
the garrison state'.

How would the specialists on violence deal with this challenge?
Physical terror and coërcion were the most obvious answer and
indeed, so Lasswell argued, 'the elite of the garrison state will have
a professional interest in multiplying gadgets specialized to acts of
violence'. But there was also the control through psychological terror
by means of war scares. At the same time he assumed that there would
be 'a rise in the production of non-military consumption goods despite
the amount of energy directed toward the production of military
equipment'. For there were the stupendous productive potentialities
of modern science and engineering'. While this would act as a
stabilizing factor for a time, the elite would soon 'feel itself endangered
by the growing "frivolousness" of the community'. At this point they
would decide that a 'blood-letting is needed in order to preserve those
virtues of sturdy acquiescence in the regime which they so much
admire and from which they so greatly benefit'. In short, the specialists
on violence would employ a whole range of techniques to appease,
bully, terrorize, manipulate and entice the mass of the population.
Modern technology would make it all possible for them. More than
that: scientists and engineers would help them to explore further 'the
technical potentialities of modern civilization'. For they would continue
to represent 'an enormous body of specialists whose focus of attention
is entirely given over to the discovery of novel ways of utilizing nature'.

Lasswell's essay is in many ways a most remarkable piece. He was
the first systematically to investigate the impact of modern technology
on the problem of militarism. His model of the Garrison State bears a
certain similarity with Spencer's 'militant type of society'. And like the
latter, he contrasted it with another type which he called the 'business
state'. However, it is indicative of the way in which the nineteenth-
century Idea of Progress had faded away that Lasswell could not
conceive of a Spencerian progression from a militaristic to an industrial
type of society. On the contrary, he arrived at the opposite prediction
that the Business State would be overrun by the specialists on violence.
It was a prospect which, it must be added, filled Lasswell with 'repug-
nance and apprehension'. He would quite frankly have liked to defer
the coming of the Garrison State. Yet, should its advent be ultimately
unavoidable, how — he asked at the end of his article — could 'the

human costs of the Garrison State be reduced'? Might it be done, he wondered, 'if we civilianize the ruling elite'?

Such statements reveal that Lasswell was less of an outsider to a tradition of discourse than might at first glance have been presumed. This conclusion becomes even more inescapable, if one takes another article which he published in 1962 and in which he tried to reexamine his 1941 hypothesis in the light of intervening developments.[34] To begin with, he saw no reason to revise his basic propositions. On the contrary, the dawn of the nuclear and computer age after 1945 was seen by him as proof that the requirements of the global rule of the specialists on violence had come to prevail. On the other hand, an interesting shift had taken place in his position with reference to the country in which the birth of the garrison state was most imminent. In 1941, Nazi Germany had been the model which threatened the capitalist West as well as socialist Russia and had driven both of them into cooperation against Central European militarism. Now, in 1962, the Soviet Union appeared to be the society most likely to be dominated by the specialists on violence. However, there existed alarming tendencies in the Western world as well.[35] In drawing the balance-sheet, Lasswell therefore thought it improbable that man would be 'moving soon into a world relatively free of chronic threat of serious coercion'. Yet, if prospects were so bleak what, he asked, would be the policies by which 'we can maintain as many as possible of the effective institutions of a free society'? His answer: 'From the point of view of the strategy of human dignity the most promising trends to encourage are "civilianism", the movement that to a degree we can say is developing counter to "militarism".'

This was, of course, an argument that had been heard in Anglo-Saxon countries many times before. There appears to be but a slight variation in the way in which Lasswell perceived the old juxtaposition of militarism and civilianism:

> If we understand by "militarism" the permeation of an entire society by the self-serving ideology of the officer and soldier, we can speak of "civilianism" as the absorption of the military by the multivalued orientation of a society in which violent coërcion is deglamorized as an end in itself and is perceived as a regrettable concession to the persistence of variables whose magnitudes we have not as yet been able to control without paying what appears to be an excessive cost in terms of such autonomy as is possible under the cloud of chronic peril.

The idea of the submersion of the military in a 'multi-valued orientation' of society did strike a new note in the debate concerning the problem of civilian control of the military. But it also seems to explain why Lasswell developed something like a mental block against digging for the roots of the dreaded militarization of society within the structure of the American political and economic system. For that matter, he was too profoundly influenced not only by the language, but also by the traditions and thought categories of political science analysis in the United States. While the theory of totalitarianism, which gained wide acceptance in the West after 1945,[36] helped him to achieve the shift from Nazi Germany to Soviet Russia as being a proto-typical garrison state, he emerged, at the end of his reappraisal, if not as an optimist, at least as a protagonist of an 'idealist' tradition: 'The master challenge of modern politics. . . is to civilianize a garrisoning world, thereby cultivating the conditions of its eventual dissolution. The discipline acquired in the process may make it possible for mankind to accomplish what it has never been able to achieve before — namely to create and perpetuate a universal public order of human dignity.' This world, to be sure, would not be the Marxian utopia. It appears that in Lasswell's case it was rather closer to the American Dream.

Lasswell's article of 1941 was one of the milestones in the debate on militarism. For the rest of the Second World War, the concept became largely a propaganda weapon against the Axis Powers. Fascism and militarism were seen as synonyms, and after the end of the war the Allies proceeded to root out German and Japanese 'militarism'. Perhaps this policy would have been more successful, if there had been a greater consensus about what was meant by it. As this was not the case, it is not surprising that scholars should once more begin to probe into the problem of militarism and to examine the cases of Germany and Japan in particular, this time with the benefit of hindsight.[37] It is to this discussion and its political and ideological context that we shall turn in Chapter III. It represented the next stage in the long debate of the concept of militarism.

Notes

1 W. Sombart, *Händler und Helden*, Berlin 1914.
2 Quoted in M. Geyer's contribution to O. Brunner et al., eds., *Lexikon Historischer Grundbegriffe*, p.40.
3 For details see E. Assmuss, *Die publizistische Diskussion*, pp.110ff.
4 G. Pfeilschrifter, ed., *Deutsche Kultur, Katholizismus und Weltkrieg*, Freiburg 1916.
5 O. Hintze, ed., *Deutschland und der Weltkrieg*, Leipzig-Berlin 1915.
6 N. Goldmann, *Der Geist des Militarismus*, Stuttgart 1915.
7 Ibid., p.8.
8 On the Western, especially British, reaction and its long-term effects upon policy-making in the interwar period see J.M. Winter, 'Britain's "Lost Generation" of the First World War.' *Population Studies* 3(1977), pp.449-66. See also: E.J. Leed, *No Man's Land*, Cambridge 1979.
9 See, e.g., W.E. Williams, *Paramilitarism in Inter-State Relations, The Role of Political Armies in Twentieth-Century Politics*, PhD. dissertation, University of London, 1965, for details.
10 By now monographs have appeared on the most important para-military associations, such as the *Stahlhelm, SA, Jungdeutscher Orden, Reichsbanner, Rotfrontkämpferbund*. For a recent overall assessment of the phenomenon in English see J.M. Diehl, *Para-military Politics in Weimar Germany*, Bloomington 1977.
11 W.E. Williams, *Paramilitarism*, pp.59ff.
12 The annual Front Soldiers' Days of the *Stahlhelm* association tended to set the standard in terms of organizational precision and military style. See V.R. Berghahn, *Der Stahlhelm, Bund der Frontsoldaten, 1918-1935*, Düsseldorf 1966, pp.55ff.
13 For a more detailed discussion of these ideas see ibid., pp.91 ff. See also K. Rohe, *Das Reichsbanner Schwarz Rot Gold*, Düsseldorf 1966, p.83ff.; H.-P. Schwarz, *Der konservative Anarchist*, Freiburg 1962, also for the following.
14 E. Jünger, *Die totale Mobilmachung*, Berlin 1930.
15 E. Jünger, *Der Arbeiter. Herrschaft und Gestalt*, Hamburg 1932.
16 Quoted in H.-P. Schwarz, *Der konservative Anarchist*, p.69.
17 H. Hansen [F. W. Heinz?], 'Patriotendämmerung.' *Die Standarte* 7 (1926), p.10.
18 Quoted in V.R. Berghahn, *Stahlhelm*, p.98.
19 For details see K. Rohe, *Reichsbanner*, pp.110ff. The founding of the *Reichsbanner* and the *Rotfrontkämpferbund* in 1924 raises the problem of a 'Red militarism' which will be discussed below pp. 85ff. Most analysts would agree with Rohe who sees the left-wing paramilitary organizations of the Weimar period as responses to the right-wing *Wehrverbände* and stresses their defensive nature as well as their subordination to party policy.
20 F. Sternthal, 'Was ist Militarismus?' *Der Neue Merkur* (1921), p.420.
21 F.C. Endres, 'Soziologische Struktur und ihr entsprechende Ideologien des deutschen Offizierkorps vor dem Weltkriege.' *Archiv für Sozialwissenschaft und Sozialpolitik* 57 (1927), pp.291ff.
22 [F.C. Endres], *Die Tragödie Deutschlands*, Stuttgart 1925, p.60.
23 Quoted by Endres in V.R. Berghahn, ed., *Militarismus*, p.99.
24 See esp. E. Kehr's article on 'Die Genesis des Königlich-Preussischen Reser-

veoffiziers', reprinted in H.-U. Wehler, ed., *Der Primat der Innenpolitik*, Berlin 1970, pp. 53ff. English transl. of Kehr's essays now available: G.A. Craig, ed., *Economic Interest, Militarism and Foreign Policy*, University of California Press 1977.

25　H.-E. Fick, *Der deutsche Militarismus der Vorkriegszeit*, LLD dissertation, University of Rostock, 1930.

26　Ibid., p.17.

27　W. Reich, *Die Funktion des Orgasmus*, Cologne 1969.

28　A. Vagts, *A History of Militarism*. The American edition appeared in New York in 1937, the English edition a year later in London. The book was sub-titled 'Romance and Realities of a Profession'. The English edition will be used for the following.

29　For details see M. Geyer's contribution to O. Brunner et al., eds., *Lexikon Historischer Grundbegriffe*, p.42.

30　Ibid. See also below pp. 111ff.

31　H.D. Lasswell, 'The Garrison State and the Specialists on Violence.' *American Journal of Sociology* (January 1941), pp.455-68.

32　See above p. 10.

33　H.D. Lasswell, 'The Garrison State', p.455, also for the following.

34　H.D. Lasswell, 'The Garrison State Hypothesis Today,' in S.P. Huntington, ed., *Changing Patterns of Military Politics*, New York 1962, pp. 51-70.

35　In this context Lasswell was particularly worried about the younger generation and advanced a somewhat peculiar pessimistic argument concerning the ego-centricity and sexual extremism of the young. Ibid., p.63.

36　H. Arendt, *The Origins of Totalitarianism*, London 1951; C.J. Friedrich and Z.K. Brzesinski, *Totalitarian Dictatorship and Autocracy*, Cambridge (Mass.) 1956, as two classic statements.

37　As far as I was able to make out, there was a lively debate on Italian Fascism in postwar Italy, but none on militarism.

III The Debate on German and Japanese Militarism

Among the objectives on which the Allies were able to agree during the Second World War, the complete disarmament and demilitarization of Germany was always considered axiomatic. These objectives were reaffirmed at the Potsdam Conference of the Big Four in the summer of 1945 and published in the *Official Gazette* of the Allied Control Council on 2 August 1945. The directive read:

> a) All German land, naval and air forces, the SS, SA, SD and Gestapo, with all their organizations, staffs and institutions, including the General Staff, the Officers' Corps, Reserve Corps, military schools, war veterans' organizations and all other military and quasi-military organization, together with all clubs and associations which serve to keep alive the military tradition in Germany, shall be completely and finally abolished in such a manner as permanently to prevent the revival or reorganization of German militarism and Nazism.
> b) All arms, ammunition and implements of war and all specialized facilities for their production shall be held at the disposal of the Allies or destroyed. The maintenance and production of all aircraft and all arms, ammunition and implements of war shall be prevented.[1]*

When these principles were enunciated, their implementation by the military authorities in the four zones of occupation was already in full swing. It was not too difficult a task as long as the problem was seen primarily as an institutional and organizational one: most of the associations and organizations had collapsed in May 1945, if not before, and arms production had also come to a complete halt. In line with the traditional Marxist interpretation which viewed militarism and National Socialism as an out-growth of capitalism, the Soviet Occupation authorities were included to let the problem rest there, now that a restructuring of (East) German society according to socialist principles had begun. To put it differently, the Soviet Union was not too concerned about militarism as a deep-rooted ideology which supposedly dominated the thinking of the mass of Germans because it approached the phenomenon from the view-point of socio-economic structure. It was assumed that the establishment of socialism would take care of the threat of militarism and Nazism.

However, as we have seen above, the non-Marxist debate had always been more preoccupied with militarism as a state of mind. And as militarism was not only presumed to have a long tradition in Germany, but also to have become an integral and all-pervasive element of Nazi indoctrination, Anglo-Saxon attitudes towards the chances of a militarist revival were bound to differ fundamentally from Soviet ones. To the Americans in particular every German was potentially, if not actually, a thorough-bred militarist and Nazi. Militarism and National Socialism were believed to have been too deeply ingrained in German culture for this to be otherwise. The wholesale de-Nazification and de-militarization and the subsequent re-education of the German population were but the logical conclusion drawn from this interpretation. This is not the place to examine the procedures which were instituted in the Western zones of occupation resulting in the political screening of millions of Germans.[2] The important point for our analysis is that a programme which involved a vast operation of ideological purification would, almost inevitably, rekindle the old debate on the basic character of militarism and German militarism in particular.

This debate started almost as soon as the printing presses began to run again. One of the first scholars to raise his voice was Friedrich Meinecke, probably the most eminent among the German historians of the older generation.[3] In 1946, he published a book, entitled *The German Catastrophe*[4], in which he tried to draw up a balance-sheet of some two hundred years of German history. Considering Meinecke's background and earlier writings, it was in many ways a blunt and remarkable assessment — at least as far as the problem of Prusso-German militarism was concerned. Here Meinecke made a straight connection between the period of Frederick William I of Prussia and the Third Reich. The Prussian Army, he wrote, 'produced a curiously penetrating militarism which affected the whole of civilian life and found no comparable expression in any of [Germany's] neighbour states'. A closer look at Meinecke's arguments reveals that he found two themes particularly noteworthy.

The first was militarism as an outgrowth of the age of science and rational planning. To him Prussian militarism 'such as was created by Frederick William I', was a precursor of the 'modern technical-utilitarian spirit', which he also regarded as an important feature of

Hitlerism. This habit of studying and treating military matters with scientific exactitude and cold-blooded rationality had, he believed, spread in the nineteenth century. It was in this milieu that 'the central organ of Prusso-German militarism was formed. . .: the Grand General Staff'. This body became the focus of all militaristic qualities and embodied them in their purest form. 'The sharp eyes of our enemies', he added with reference to Allied wartime arguments, 'have not without reason seen the quintessence of our militarism in this General Staff and now [after 1945] made it their task to root it out completely'.

Yet, beside the rational aspect of militarism there was, according to Meinecke, an irrational one which came to bear after the First World War: the intoxication of the *younger* generation with nationalistic and militaristic 'ideals'. The young, he argued, had given their blind support to National Socialism. This in itself did not bring the Nazis to power, however. Rather 'the fate of the Hitler movement rested in large measure on the behaviour and ethos of the Reichswehr' whose officer corps was poorly equipped to see through the rhetoric of National Socialist propaganda. This naiveté, Meinecke asserts, was in turn 'closely related to the one-sidedness of Prusso-German militarism with its highly developed technical ethos and its emphasis on narrow military expertise'. In short, in 1933 the two currents underlying German militarism merged to produce a regime led by Hitler, whose policies were to prove 'catastrophic' to the country and Europe as a whole.

In the same year in which Meinecke published *The German Catastrophe*, another well-known historian, Hans Herzfeld, devoted an article to the theme of German militarism.[5] He agreed with the former that the technological aspect of modern militarism was very important. But he warned against tracing it back too far into the past and thus blurring the issues. It was through rationalization and automation that forces had been unleashed which 'no earlier epoch has experienced'. The result was 'an unfolding of destructive capabilities which were striving beyond the limits of the imaginable'. In one sense, Herzfeld continued, militarism was therefore 'the increased perfection of all the possibilities of military organization'. However, it was also the penetration of military thinking into the sphere of politics. For this reason he insisted upon drawing a clear dividing-line between militarism and 'soldierdom'.

Finally, Herzfeld tried to place the problem into a broader context of European history by pointing out that the notion of militarism, though not the word, had first arisen in England in the seventeenth century and that it had subsequently bedevilled other European nations and France in particular. In a way Meinecke and Herzfeld were doing no more than to combine the arguments of Vagts and Lasswell. Above all, they tried to place the phenomenon of militarism into a European context, and that was a most unpopular approach in 1946. Certainly it was not only out of tune with Allied assumptions and their policy of de-Nazification and de-militarization, but also with what Western historians were writing on this subject. In Britain, scholars like Alan J.P. Taylor and John Wheeler-Bennett stressed that uniqueness of German militarism and then traced it back as far as the early modern period.[6] Some, like William Shirer, even claimed that militarism was endemic in the German national character.

It was from a position of defiant disbelief that the American historian Gordon A. Craig began his research into *The Politics of the Prussian Army, 1640-1945* which he published in book-form in 1955.[7] He did not deny 'that authoritarian government, militarism and aggression have characterized German political life and action in the modern period'. But, he added, 'to assign national characteristics to a people is at best a chancy business and arguments based upon such attribution are apt to fall of their own weight'. He believed that it was a sounder research strategy to assume that, 'as [the American political scientist] Franz Neumann has written — [militarism and aggression were] "products of a structure which vitiated attempts to create a viable democracy"'. Although the juxtaposition was not new, Craig's book nevertheless deserves mention, not least because he presented a good deal of empirical evidence in support of his structural analysis. One of his hypotheses was the notion that 'technical progress' and 'the progressive mechanization of warfare' had changed the relationship between the military and civilians since the nineteenth century. This he thought was particularly true of foreign relations, where after 1870 policy-makers in all European countries had found it 'essential. . ., in time of international tension, to solicit and weigh the advice of army and navy staffs concerning foreign capabilities'.

However, the dangers inherent in this reliance on military advice were always recognised 'in the democratic states' in which the civilian authorities consistently tried to make certain that the ultimate decision rested with them. Bismarck's successors by contrast were 'less effective than he in keeping the military within bounds. In consequence, the Wilhelmine era was characterized by the progressive usurpation by the military agencies of the authority and functions of the professional diplomats. Operational plans for future wars, were adopted, for instance, in a form which seriously limited the diplomatic freedom of the state. . .'

No less fateful was, in Craig's view, that 'the policy of the army was a decisive factor in the domestic history of Germany in the nineteenth century'. The main purpose of the book was to demonstrate that there existed strong forces of change towards a liberal society and civilian government in nineteenth-century Central Europe, but that these forces had been repeatedly thwarted by the Army. Thus liberalism failed to advance not because there were no liberals, but because the balance of forces and the support by the Army of the *status quo* tipped the scales in favour of conservatism at certain crucial moments in history. In the 1930s, on the other hand, when a policy of reaction would have been in the interest of the Army, the officer corps failed to react. Much of Craig's study is therefore devoted to explaining the apparent paradox of why the Army was so stubborn when it would have been wiser to be flexible and why, in the 1930s, it was flexible when it would have been more than appropriate to resist Hitler. The picture which he painted of the German military amounted to an indictment with which Meineccke and Herzfeld would probably have concurred. But by the time Craig's book appeared, influential German historians had taken up a different position and unleashed a major controversy on the whole problem of militarism.

In order fully to appreciate the underlying causes of this shift two points must be borne in mind. The first is that German historians had always seen themselves as teachers of the nation. Before 1914, they had been in the forefront of instilling the public, through their writings and lectures, with a belief in the achievements of the Hohenzollern monarchy (including its army) and with pride in the greatness of German culture, the educational system and the country's dynamic economic organization.[8] During the First World War, as we have seen in Chapter II, most of them became ardent advocates of a *Siegfrieden*. During the interwar period they expended much energy persuading people at home and abroad that Germany was innocent of causing the outbreak of war in 1914. There was hardly anyone who, in one way or another, did not take a stand on the so-called war guilt question. After 1933, then, all too many of them made their peace with the National Socialists who were only too pleased to accept their services. Historians were now expected to show that the Third Reich was nothing less than the culmination of several hundred years of German history.[9]

Gerhard Ritter argued in his biography of Frederik II that there existed a continuity which ran from the famous Prussian king straight to Hitler, adding:[10] 'And the Day of Potsdam [in March 1933], the solemn inauguration of the "Third Reich", established the formal link with the proudest traditions of Old-Prussian history'. A sense of mission, the feeling that they were the teachers of the German public, did not disappear with the 'collapse' of 1945. The strength of this tradition was reinforced by another factor. By and large most German historians succeeded remarkably well in negotiating the transition to the postwar period. Thus, when the universities opened their doors again in 1945/46, the tradition of national pedagogy was quickly revived.

The other point to be remembered is that these professors found in front of them students, many of them in their late twenties, who had spent their most important formative years under the influence of Nazi propaganda and had experienced five years of total war; many of them had been at the front and quite a few returned as invalids. Their world of ideas and beliefs had collapsed; more than one of them had become totally cynical about politics and lived in an ideological vacuum. At the same time they were most eager to learn and to build their personal career. The general situation looked very bleak indeed. German history professors saw themselves surrounded by a society in a state of chaos. Millions had lost their home and their belongings. It appeared as if occupied Germany was a society of uprooted people without a future and, perhaps worse, without a sense of the past. Would these 'masses' not become easy prey to radical ideas unless they were provided with a more 'positive' view of their history than what the Allies were offering? And was it not the duty of the country's intellectual leaders to contribute their own interpretation of the horrific events of the past? Was this not the only basis on which a stable society might be reconstructed, bearing in mind the argument that a society without History is like an individual without memory? And finally, would a society whose history consisted of nothing else but a series of disasters not be just as open to dangerous ideologies as a society without any sense of History? Certainly, the 'facts' of Nazi criminality had to be told. However, much depended upon the interpretation that was put upon these 'facts'. Even granted that the Third Reich had been a nightmare, was it possible and, for that matter, 'responsible' to say that the whole of modern German history was an uninterrupted series of nightmares?

Faced with these awkward questions, most German historians adopted a view whose simplicity cannot fail to impress: they cut the Third Reich out of the mainstream of German history and proclaimed that it had been no more than an unfortunate 'accident in the works' (*Betriebsunfall*).[11] It is no exaggeration to say that this became a widely accepted interpretation among West Germans. Meanwhile children in East Germany grew up with an orthodox Marxist view of pre-1945 history.[12] The notion, implicit in the *Betriebsunfall* theory, that 1933 constituted a fundamental break in German history also facilitated the demonization of the Hitler period. Germany, the argument ran, had been taken over in 1933 by a gang of criminals who had descended upon a highly civilized country almost out of the blue. To Ludwig Dehio, a friend of Meinecke and editor of the time-honoured *Historische Zeitschrift*, Hitler was the 'demon incarnate', a 'satanic genius'.[13] Dehio's views are significant also because he was one of the few academics of the older generation who modified his position on certain other aspects of German history.

The bone of contention between him and his colleagues was his evaluation of the basic character of the Prusso-German military state. This was the issue over which he came to blows with Ritter who, after Meinecke's death in 1953, was undoubtedly the most influential among West Germany's professional historians. In the late 1940s and early 1950s, Ritter had been in the forefront of those interpreters of the past to whom the year 1933 represented the great discontinuity in German history. In 1953, then, he gave his appraisal of German militarism at the XXII Congress of German Historians in Bremen. By the end of this lecture, it was abundantly clear that the thrust of his argument was very different from that of Meinecke and Herzfeld some seven years earlier.[14] The immediate stimulus for Ritter's lecture was provided by the public debate on German rearmament, and it is not difficult to see why this issue, which arose so soon after the country had been demilitarized, should generate a good deal of heat. For Ritter it provided first of all a good opportunity to reaffirm the pedagogical function of historical writing: 'It is an essential task of political history to define, by looking back into the past, the historical position in which we find ourselves at present and thus to ease the task of the practical politician; only he who knows the ground relatively well on which he moves will be able to take firm steps into the future.'

Ritter then proceeded to define militarism. He argued that it contained two elements which were not to be confused with military matters:

1) 'The onesided determination of political decisions by military-technical considerations replacing a comprehensive examination of what is required by *raison d'état*' — which comprised both the military aspect of state policy as well as the moral code.

2) 'The onesided predominance of militant and martial traits in a stateman's or nation's basic political outlook' to the extent that the most important task of a state is neglected,

which is 'to create a durable order of law and peace among
men, to promote general welfare and mediate continuously
in the eternal struggle among divergent interests and
claims in domestic affairs and between nations'.

The conservatism of Ritter's position, as reflected in these words, and
the narrowness of his definition of militarism hardly require further
comment. The rest of the lecture reinforces this point; for these were
the yardsticks which Ritter now proceeded to apply to German history.
The policies of the Prussian kings, he maintained, could not be called
'militaristic' since the Prussian army continued to adhere to an ethos of
'sober soldierdom'. By the 1860s, he admitted, a number of 'militarists'
had emerged around the court. But Bismarck, whom Ritter portrays as
'the last great cabinet politician of Europe', was able to assert his
position. He blocked a shift towards a 'militaristic' *foreign* policy, as
Ritter had defined it.

It was only in the post-Bismarckian period and partly under the
impact of rapid changes in weapons' technology and the growth of
highly organized mass armies, that politicians began to lose control.
During the same period, he continued, the 'nation' likewise changed
its basic outlook from that of the early nineteenth century. Ritter
believed that it was wrong to regard the idealistic war enthusiasm of
the struggle against Napoleon as a form of 'militarism'. Nor would it be
right to equate a positive attitude towards military service with a
martial spirit. It was only just before and after 1914 that the desire
to work for international peace and order became submerged in a
destructive orgy of xenophobia and chauvinist hysteria.

Thus the dominance of technical factors and martial popular passions
conspired to produce the militaristic policy of the late Wilhelmine
period. It was during the First World War, he continued, that the fatal
preponderance of the soldier over the politician became irreversible.
To Ritter, General Erich Ludendorff, the 'silent dictator' of Germany,[15]
was an 'arch militarist of the purest kind'. German militarism reached
the final stage of its development in the early 1930s. Yet the collapse of
the Weimar Republic was not ushered in 'by the "militarists" of the
Army'; it was caused 'by the militarism of the National Socialist
people's movement'. Even now Ritter was unwilling 'simply and without qualification' to call 'these civilian supporters of Hitler militarists'.
While Ritter did not hesistate to regard Hitler as 'the most extreme of
all militarists', he took a different view of 'the great mass of those who
cheered the dangerous demagogue': they 'did not expect a new war of
him', but the unification of a polarized society. In addition they longed

for the re-establishment of Germany's prestige and position in the world.

Ritter's address of 1953 exerted a major influence upon the debate on militarism, at least in so far as it was conducted inside West Germany. His hypotheses were bound to strike a responsive chord among the country's political elites who were by then trying to convince a reluctant population of the need for German rearmament. The lecture and its publication in *Historische Zeitschrift* was followed by a book entitled *Staatskunst und Kriegshandwerk*.[16] It was the first of a multi-volume project designed to support his arguments with detailed historical material. Its sub-title: 'The Problem of "Militarism" in Germany' — militarism in inverted commas. The volume which had reached its third impression by 1965, began with the statement:[17] 'The problem of "militarism" is the problem of the correct relationship between statecraft and the technique of warfare. Militarism is an exaltation and over-estimation of soldierdom which turns the relationship into an unhealthy state of affairs.' Seen in this perspective, Ritter added, '"militarism" is the extreme opposite of "pacifism"'. In this way militarism was defined by him as a problem of foreign policy and of the modern state, detached from that state's social and economic structures. In so far as Ritter was prepared to consider social factors at all, they made their appearance in the shape of the 'masses' of the democratic age.

It was a change of emphasis whose significance can hardly be over-estimated: militarism had now explicitly become the product of the French Revolution and the advent of mass politics. It was hence everything else but a Prusso-German invention. This argument was too seductive and comforting not to be given a warm welcome among Ritter's colleagues, the more so as its anti-Western sting could be deflected with the help of the by then popular theory of totalitarianism. Writing in 1954 in *Geschichte in Wissenschaft und Unterricht*, the journal of the Association of History Masters, Werner Picht came to the following conclusion:[18] 'It is precisely the appearance and zealous spreading of a totalitarian militarism as a symptom of the age of the masses and as an expression of the world revolution of the proletariat which throws the different nature of German militarism into sharp relief.' If, he continued, one wished to employ the concept at all, German militarism had been aristocratic, territorially limited, modest and pledged to the upholding of a soldierly ethos.

The only influential historian of the older generation to object to Ritter's analysis was Dehio. In 1955 he wrote a lengthy review article of *Staatskunst und Kriegshandwerk* for the journal of which he was the

editor.[19] His argument amounted to a vigorous denial of Ritter's
central point concerning the discontinuity of 1933. He also raised
serious questions about Ritter's view that there existed a dichotomy
between a policy guided by *raison d'état* and one propelled by
militarism. In effect, the *raison d'état* of the Prussian state, he argued,
had been militaristic since the eighteenth century. It was this tradition,
Dehio maintained, that had made it possible for an unknown territorial
entity called Prussia to grow into a formidable continental power. The
same tradition was said to be responsible for Germany's late-nine-
teenth-century drive for overseas possessions which followed the
creation, in 1871, of a national state and a society instilled with 'a faith
in armaments, discipline and autocratic leadership'. In the end Dehio
found it impossible 'to suppress his concern' that Ritter, by introducing
his 'narrow definition of *raison d'état*', had blocked the access to the
'hardcore of what is the real German militarism'.

Dehio never succeeded in clearing away the arguments which Ritter
had put forward. The debate continued to be fought out on Ritter's
terms and with Ritter's terminology. It centred on the problem of
whether Frederick II or Bismarck had conducted a militaristic foreign
policy. As long as diplomacy and individuals attracted all the attention, other interesting questions which tried to relate the issue of
militarism to the structure of Prusso-German society were never even
broached. Otto Büsch made an attempt, in his 1953 PhD. thesis, to
move away from diplomatic history into the field of social history when
he examined the beginnings of what he called the 'social militarization'
of Prussian society in the eighteenth century. But he was a young man
and his study remained unpublished until 1962.[20]

By that time, Fritz Fischer had published his by now famous study
on *Germany's War Aims in the First World War*.[21] Although not
directly concerned with the problem of militarism, this book marked a
watershed between quite different approaches to the study of modern
German history. In raising the question of German responsibility for
the outbreak of the First World War and by providing detailed archival
material concerning the nature of German expansionism during the
war, Fischer gave a fresh impetus to the discussion of the continuities
in German history. Unlike Dehio, who had countered Ritter's points
with equally sweeping statements on the evolution and character of
Prusso-German power politics, Fischer presented fresh empirical
evidence which it was difficult to refute. Above all, his findings
encouraged historians of the younger generation to ask questions
which Ritter and other scholars who dominated the historical profession in West Germany in the 1950s had chosen to ignore.[22]

These younger historians took it for granted that Dehio's criticism of Ritter was essentially accurate and began to wonder whether the roots of those '200 years of militaristic politics', as Dehio had put it, might not be found in the socio-economic power structures of Prussia-Germany. They became particularly interested in the impact of industrialization upon a 'backward' society and a (semi-)autocratic political system. They focused on the functionality of militarism and its role as a stabilizing factor in a society which had become exposed to rapid economic change.[23] Finally, these younger historians also wanted to know precisely who those militarized 'masses' were and what it was that had militarized them. The end-result of this changing academic interest has been that the phenomenon of Prusso-German militarism is no longer being studied in the context in which Ritter saw it, but is approached today with the tools of analysis of the social scientist and social historian. Kehr's essays of the 1920s were re-discovered and republished,[24] and so were Marx and Max Weber whose methodologies had been explicitly rejected by Ritter and many of his colleagues in the 1950s. Another outcome of this 'revolution in German historiography'[25] was that the research interests of Marxist and non-Marxist historians ceased to diverge as dramatically as they had done in the early postwar period.

As might be expected, the East German discussion of the problem of militarism had revolved around issues very different from those which agitated Ritter. To begin with, a regime had been installed in what was at first the Soviet zone of occupation which proclaimed to have made (and in many ways did make) a radical break with the past. In the East there emerged a system which was supposed to be very different from all previous political and social organizations that had existed in Central Europe. The year 1945 was hence seen as the great divide in German history and East German historians were not motivated by a desire to discover other watersheds, as Meinecke and Ritter had been. Marxism-Leninism-Stalinism provided a framework of analysis to which everybody had to subscribe, but it produced an interpretation of the German past which made the agonizing search for an acceptable tradition quite unnecessary. The tradition was that of the German working class and its struggle against militarism, a struggle in which Ritter, significantly enough, had never been seriously interested.

Marxism-Leninism, as adopted by East German historians, also simplified the discussion of militarism as a historical problem. We have seen in Chapter I how Marxist analysts had reached a large measure of agreement about the nature of militarism before 1914. The basic approach remained unchanged in subsequent decades and it is not surprising that Liebknecht's interpretation of 1906 should form a central reference point of much of what East German historians wrote on the subject.[26] When Alfred Meusel published a reply to Ritter's 1953 lecture in the East German *Zeitschrift für Geschichtswissenschaft*, he quoted Engels, Liebknecht, Lenin, Luxemburg and Franz Mehring.[27] In 1956 the political theorist Ernst Engelberg intervened in the West German debate with an article in which he scored a number of perfectly fair, though predictable, points against Ritter.[28] What, of course, he missed most in Ritter's address was a 'genuine analysis of class relations'. Militarism, he continued, resulted 'from the social and political predominance of the most reactionary elements of the exploiting classes'. In the old days, these classes were represented by 'the most reactionary parts of the feudal aristocracy' and 'today by the most reactionary parts of the imperialistic bourgeoisie'.

If this periodization of the incidence of militarism is to be taken literally, it would appear to imply a shift away from Liebknecht. As will be remembered, the latter had considered Wilhelmine Germany the 'paradigm' of a capitalist militarism. Engelberg, on the other hand, was apparently more prepared than Liebknecht to admit that Prusso-German militarism was influenced by powerful pre-industrial groups which dominated pre-1914 German politics. Engelberg thus anticipated a trend in East German historiography which gained ground in the 1960s and which has tended to stress the 'relative backwardness' of the Wilhelmine Empire. Although they were still miles apart in other respects, East and West German historians had, as a result of the shifts that had taken place on both sides by the late 1960s, reached a common starting-point from which they were at least able to talk to each other. Socio-economic structures, not questions of *raison d'état* provided the meeting-ground. Interestingly enough, it was the same basis around which the discussion of Japanese militarism came to revolve after 1945. The rest of this chapter will therefore be concerned with the case of this Far Eastern society in so far as it sheds light on our topic.

Japan capitulated on 15 August 1945. A regime collapsed which had become classified as 'militaristic' in much the same way as Nazi Germany. The Allies set out to demolish Japanese militarism and to introduce Western political values and institutions.[29] As in Central Europe, there existed a number of plans for dealing with the defeated nation and its leaders, among which the Australian proposals were the most punitive. The American approach, on the other hand, was more selective and tended to focus on the question of what should be done with the Japanese elites and above all with the Emperor himself.

According to the Potsdam Declaration on Japan, there were to be 'removed for all time the authority and influence of those who deceived and misled the people of Japan into embarking upon world conquest, for we insist that the new order of peace, security and justice will be impossible until irresponsible militarism is driven from the world'.[30] In particular, the Americans were much less inclined than they had been in the case of Germany to administer the country collectively together with their Allies. Disagreements which resulted from this attitude were ultimately resolved by the appointment of General Douglas MacArthur who, for the next five years and with President Harry Truman's backing, was 'to rule absolute in Japan' and 'to disregard almost all suggestions from other Allied governments'.[31]

Although the Allies approached the two defeated countries differently, the psychological situation of the Japanese was not dissimilar from that of the Germans in 1945 as they looked back upon their history and tried to interpret the past. Almost inevitably, they began to ask themselves the same kinds of questions which intellectuals and academics were raising in Germany about their own history. One of the arguments advanced was that the regime which had been responsible for the outbreak of the war in the Far East and the collapse of Japanese power four years later had no connection with the country's culture and institutions. Fascism and militarism were said to have descended upon the country out of the blue. This view was complemented in the early 1950s by the hypothesis that Japanese Fascism had been a product of mass society and 'democratic' politics.[32] It is difficult to say if these interpretations were influenced by what German historians were writing at this time about the Nazi past. All we know is that Meinecke's *The German Catastrophe* and Ritter's *Die Dämonie der Macht (The Demonic Nature of Power)* were translated into Japanese 'very early and very soon reached a wide readership'.[33]

Yet it would be wrong to give the impression that these views ever achieved the same respectability which they gained in West Germany. From the outset, there was a much greater preparedness to ask fundamental questions about Japan's development and to respond positively to the reforms which began to affect all spheres of life. Especially in the universities the forces opposed to an unreconstructed conservatism were much stronger than in Germany and the works of Hisao Otsuka and Masao Maruyama enjoyed considerable authority.[34] Marxist interpretations of twentieth-century Japanese history were also popular and found support among the working class, the urban white-collar workers and students. Inevitably and under the influence of a radical professoriat, questions of socio-economic structure were at the centre of interest and although they approached the problem from various angles, the debate among left-wing scholars tended to focus on the problem of Japan's 'backwardness' and its impact on her political development.

However, the actual stimulus to analyse the evolution of modern Japan in these terms was indirectly provided by the prewar writings of Otsuka (who, in turn, had been influenced by Eitaro Noro and Moritaro Yamada). An expert in English and European economic history, he had argued in the 1930s that the dissolution of feudalism had produced an Anglo-American and an East Elbian type of social organization. Whereas the former had led to the gradual erosion of the power positions of agriculture, the latter had secured the survival of traditional agrarian elites and had blocked the path towards a parliamentary-civilian system of the Western type. Whether or not Otsuka's theory of the two roads towards modernity, a 'Prussian' and an 'American' one, was indebted to Marx and Lenin, it certainly exerted a considerable influence on his pupils. They added force to this interpretation in a number of highly interesting studies which examined the socio-economic and political problems of the 'underdeveloped' regions of Europe. What, they asked themselves, were the 'relics' of feudalism in emerging capitalist-industrial societies and how did they influence the development of these societies? And all the time the evolution of Japan was, of course, at the back of their minds.

Whereas the Otsuka School was primarily interested in European economic history, Maruyama's important contributions are explicitly *comparatiste* and included the analysis of the Japanese situation. It was in this context that he also came to write about the role of fascism and militarism. Finally, on the extreme left, Communist intellectuals debated divergent Marxist approaches to the problem. But whatever their differences, even the Leninist-influenced *Kozaha* — and this is significant for our purposes — refused to see the dictatorship of the 'fascist' period as an outgrowth of a developed capitalist economy and stressed the 'backward' features of the regime. Only the *Ronoha* took up a different position. Nevertheless, there developed a broad consensus between a number of groups that the best way into the subject of modern Japanese history was not via politics and ideology, but via the country's political economy. The regime of the 1930s and 1940s was hence not seen as a product of the monopoly phase of capitalism, but of 'underdevelopment'. If there was a difference in interpretation, it was about the character and social base of German *National Socialism* which the *Kozaha* was inclined to associate with advanced capitalism. The Japanese experience of fascism, on the other hand, was agreed to be a case of 'relative backwardness'.

This meant that the Japanese debate on the problem of militarism was much less circuitous than the German one and concentrated quite early on upon the functionality of the phenomenon. However, it must in fairness be added that there was much more overwhelming empirical evidence favouring an 'instrumentalist' approach and making nonsense of the 'demonic' and 'democratic' argument, as a brief discussion of Japanese history will show. Any account of modern Japan will mention the year 1868 as an important date; yet few would view this year, which initiated the fall of feudalism, as a major divide. On the contrary, the social and political power base of the so-called Meji Restoration was provided by a small traditional elite which had been running the country before and now continued to run it within a different constitutional framework. The interesting point for our analysis is that this elite rested upon a system of military clans among which the *Choshu* and the *Satsuma* clans held the key positions. These clans used 'the *taiken* [the absolutist powers of the Tenno] as a basis for dictatorial powers and monopolized the direction of politics by concentrating powers in the hands of cliques to which they themselves belonged'.[35] Their ethos continued to be that of the *samurai* of the feudal period. It was enshrined in the concept of *bushido* which another Japanese historian has defined as a 'code of militarism'.[36] While this code pervaded the political attitudes and thinking of the cliques, their influence was buttressed by the structure of the Constitution. Under the Constitution of 1889, the Emperor held the supreme command of the army and the navy. In effect this meant that the military sphere was removed from the rest of the political system and became an independent element — the other half of what was called 'dual government'. Japan thus had two governmental spheres, unified only by the person of the Emperor. It was an arrangement which virtually guaranteed the military a decisive say in policy-making.[37]

The peculiar construction of the Constitution was to assume growing significance in the interwar period when a party system established itself and civilian leaders succeeded in gaining a voice in the cabinet. This development made the Army and Navy leadership even more aware than before of the need to shield the military command sphere from civilian control and to preserve their influence on government policy through the nomination of high-ranking officers as ministers for the armed forces. Tensions between the military and the politicians were the inevitable consequence. By the early 1930s, conflicts between the two spheres of 'dual government' had become so serious that the Army was preparing plans, within its own domain, for foreign military expansion as a means of preventing the existing constitutional system from slithering into parliamentarism. The idea was to erect *soryokusen taisei* (a 'total war order') reminiscent in some respects of Lasswell's Garrion State and possibly inspired by Ludendorff's theory of total mobilization. At the same time a number of young officers combined to form the *Sakura kai* (Cherry Society) which began to make serious preparations for a *coup d'état*. A number of dangerous crises resulted from the constant plotting of the Army and Navy. Naval officers were at the centre of the May 1932 Incident. One of the Army factions, the *Kodoha*, was behind the so-called Incident of 26 February 1936; yet another group of Army officers, the *Toseiha*, tried to exploit the resulting instability to establish a military dictatorship. The increasing intervention of the military in government affairs was reflected in a mushrooming of military societies such as the *Teikoku Gunjin Engokai* (Imperial Association for the Aid of Veterans), the *Teikoku Zaigo Gunjinkai* (Veterans' Association) and the *Kokusaku Kenkyu Doshikai* (Association for the Promotion of National Defence).[38] Although there existed a strong and fairly well-organized counter-movement both inside and outside the socialist organizations, it was pushed back step-by-step, and by the end of the 1930s Japan was for all practical purposes a highly militarized society in which the Army and the Navy called the tune.

The influence of the military in Japanese politics and society after 1868 was so blatantly obvious that most historians never agonized as much as the Germans over the applicability of the concept of militarism.[39] There was no debate comparable to that between Ritter and Dehio. The path was thus clear for an analysis of the social and political structures that lay behind the militarization of Japanese foreign and domestic affairs. And if the results of this research are drawn together, the area of agreement is remarkably wide: Japanese militarism was seen as one among several devices by which an elite of officers, bureaucrats, landowners and bankers tried to cement the existing political and economic order and hence its own existence against the tide of change. It was an approach which Ritter had always refused to adopt, but which has inspired the debate not only in Japan, but also the discussion concerning the position of the military in the Developing World. It is to this latter debate, which began slightly later than the controversies about Prussia-Germany and Japan and which took place mainly among social scientists, that we must now turn. Although the latter rarely make explicit reference to the authors and arguments presented so far, the links between Chapter IV and the previous ones will, it is hoped, quickly become obvious.

Notes

1   *Protocol of the Proceedings of the Berlin Conference, 2 August 1945*, Misc. No.6 (1947), Cmd. 7087, HMSO, London 1947.
2   On the whole problem see M. Balfour, *Four-Power Control in Germany, 1945-1946*, London 1955.
3   On Meinecke see, e.g., R.A. Pois, *Friedrich Meinecke and German Politics in the Twentieth Century*, Los Angeles 1972.
4   F. Meinecke, *Die deutsche Katastrophe*, Wiesbaden 1946, English transl. under the title *The German Catastrophe*, New York 1963. The German version has been used for the following, esp. the chapter on 'Militarismus und Hitlerismus'.
5   H. Herzfeld, 'Der Militarismus als Problem', pp.41ff., also for the following.
6   See, e.g., A.J.P. Taylor, *The Course of German History*, London 1946; J. Wheeler-Bennett, *The Nemesis of Power*, London 1953.
7   London 1955, also for the following.
8   On the role of the German professoriat see F.K. Ringer, *The Decline of the German Mandarins*, Cambridge (Mass.) 1969.
9   See, e.g., F.K. Werner, *Das NS-Geschichtsbild und die deutsche Geschichtswissenschaft*, Stuttgart 1967.
10   G. Ritter, *Friedrich der Grosse*, Leipzig 1942.
11   For details see G.G. Iggers, *The German Conception of History*, Wesleyan University Press 1968.
12   It is not necessary to go into these differences, except to say that the Cold War and the ideological confrontation in Central Europe did not leave any room for a historiographical rapprochement. See also below p. 59.
13   L. Dehio, *Deutschland und die Weltpolitik im 20. Jahrhundert*, München 1955, p. 35, 30.
14   G. Ritter, 'Das Problem des Militarismus in Deutschland.' *Historische Zeitschrift* 177 (1954), pp. 21-48, also for the following.
15   See M. Kitchen, *The Silent Dictatorship*, London 1976.
16   G. Ritter, *Staatskunst und Kriegshandwerk*, Vol. 1, München 1954.
17   Ibid., p.13. Ultimately, the study ran into four volumes which were transl. into English under the title *The Sword and the Sceptre*, London 1972 ff.
18   W. Picht, 'Der Begriff "Militarismus".' *Geschichte in Wissenschaft und Unterricht* 5 (1954), p.468.
19   L. Dehio, 'Um den deutschen Militarismus.' *Historische Zeitschrift* 180 (1955 , pp. 43-64, also for the following.
20   O. Büsch, *Militärsystem und Sozialleben im alten Preussen, 1713-1807. Die Anfänge der sozialen Militarisierung der preussischen Gesellschaft*, Berlin 1962.
21   Thus the title of the English transl. of F. Fischer, *Griff nach der Weltmacht*, Düsseldorf 1961.
22   On the Fischer Controversy, its background and its impact see J.A. Moses, *The Politics of Illusion*, London 1975.
23   The most concise statement of this 'revisionist' position is contained in H.-U. Wehler, *Das deutsche Kaiserreich, 1871-1918,* Göttingen 1973. For a synthetic view of the period 1895-1914 in English see V.R. Berghahn, *Germany and the Approach of War in 1914*, London 1973.
24   See H.-U. Wehler, ed., *Der Primat der Innenpolitik*.
25   J.A. Moses, *The Politics of Illusion*, p. XI.
26   See, e.g., the entry on 'militarism' in *Marxistisch-Leninistisches Wörterbuch der*

Philosophie, Vol. 2, p. 724ff.

27 A. Meusel, 'Zum Vortrag von G. Ritter: "Das Problem des Militarismus in Deutschland".' *Zeitschrift für Geschichtswissenschaft* 1 (1953), pp. 923ff.

28 E. Engelberg, 'Über das Problem des deutschen Militarismus.' *Zeitschrift für Geschichtswissenschaft* 4 (1956), pp. 1113-45.

29 See, e.g., D. Bergamini, *Japan's Imperial Conspiracy,* London 1972, esp. pp. 115ff.

30 Quoted in W. Benz, 'Amerikanische Besatzungspolitik in Japan, 1945-47.' *Vierteljahrshefte für Zeitgeschichte* 2 (1978), pp. 265-346, 299.

31 D. Bergamini, *Japan's Imperial Conspiracy,* p. 129.

32 O. Murase, 'Nationalsozialismusforschung in Japan seit 1945', in I. Geiss and B.-J. Wendt, eds., *Deutschland in der Weltpolitik des 19. und 20. Jahrhunderts,* Düsseldorf 1973, p.540. This section is generally indebted to Professors Murase and Ohno.

33 Ibid.

34 Some of the latter's writings have appeared in English translation in M. Maruyama, *Thought and Behaviour in Modern Japanese Politics,* Oxford 1969. It would be interesting to ask how far Barrington Moore's influential book on the *Social Origins of Dictatorship and Democracy,* Cambridge (Mass.) 1966, was indebted to the Otsuka School.

35 S. Sato, 'From Party Politics to Military Dictatorship.' *The Developing Economies* 5 (1967), p. 667.

36 V. Iwasaki quoted in K.W. Colgrove, *Militarism in Japan,* Boston-New York 1936, p.5.

37 See the article by S. Seizaburo, 'From Party Politics', and the chapter on Japan in S. P. Huntington, *The Soldier and the State,* Cambridge (Mass.) 1957, pp.124ff., also for the following.

38 For details see K.W. Colgrove, *Militarism in Japan,* pp. 33ff. Other relevant studies: Y.C. Maxon, *Control of Japanese Foreign Policy. A Study of Civil-Military Rivalry, 1930-1945,* Berkeley 1957; I. Morris, ed., *Japan 1931-1945. Militarism, Fascism, Japanism?,* Boston 1963; R.J. Smethurst, *A Social Basis for Prewar Japanese Militarism. The Army and the Rural Community,* Berkeley 1974.

39 However, it may be worthwhile asking whether Japan began to develop precepts for the organization of a highly militarized society which will be analysed with reference to the Nazi system in Chapter VI below. This suggestion stems from the work of Akira Hara on war economy planning in Japan in the late 1930s and the reception of Ludendorff's ideas. Thus Japanese radio broadcast a series of five talks by Toshio Mano in November/December 1939 in which Ludendorff's concept of 'total mobilization' was discussed. See M. Miyake, 'Die Lage Japans bei Ausbruch des Zweiten Weltkriegs', in W. Benz and H. Graml, eds., *Sommer 1939,* Stuttgart 1979, p.218f.

IV Civil-Military Relations in the Third World

We have seen in the previous chapter how the debate on Prusso-German and Japanese militarism came to revolve increasingly around the notion that militarism in those countries cannot be separated from the question of their transition from an agrarian to an industrial society. In the case of Japan the relationship between 'backwardness' and militaristic tendencies was never seriously in doubt, at least not among professional historians. As far as the Prusso-German example was concerned, the view persisted much longer that its militarism was an outgrowth of the advanced state of German capitalism. Liebknecht's influence may partly explain the persistence of this interpretation. Yet in recent years, Marxist as well as non-Marxist scholars have become more and more convinced that it would be more fruitful to compare Germany with Japan rather than to put both countries into the same category of socio-economic development as Britain or the United States.[1]* It is an approach which the Berkeley historian Wolfgang Sauer propounded in his important article of 1965 when he spoke of a 'similar inner-directedness and a similar retarded development towards industrial society' which can be observed in both Japan and Germany 'despite their opposite geographical situation'.[2] He contrasted these characteristics with those of the more advanced state of the capitalist-industrial societies of the West which, he added, did not experience militaristic regimes.[3]

Seen from this perspective, the intensification of a pre-1914 militarism which occurred in Germany and Japan in the interwar period would appear to be a logical evolution of a phenomenon associated with relatively 'backward' countries. Unlike the approach which sees fascism and militarism as an outgrowth of the crisis of monopoly capitalism, this interpretation has the further advantage of being able to explain why Britain and the United States succeeded in avoiding the German and Japanese 'experiments' and why, between 1939 and 1945, these two countries found themselves allied with the Soviet Union

*The notes for this chapter begin on page 82.

against the three Axis Powers whose elites clung to the idea that the socio-economic dislocations of the interwar period could only be overcome by means of repression at home and expansionist wars abroad. From this view-point, the cases of Germany and Japan represent examples of a militarism in societies which were making their painful transition from agrarian-feudal structures and modes of political behaviour to industrial-capitalist ones. The question which we shall have to look at in this chapter is whether it is justified to apply this notion of militarism to the developing countries of the post-1945 period. After all, they too were making their transition from a pre-industrial to a 'westernized' pattern of social and political organization and were, by the same token, evidently also afflicted by major problems resulting from the weight of the military in their societies and decision-making processes.

Before surveying the literature on militarism in the Third World, three preliminary observations must be made. Firstly, few if any of the concepts used in the early postwar debate in Germany can be found in the discussions of civil-military relations in the Third World. Significantly enough, the arguments presented by Ritter and others left no trace outside the German sphere. From the start, most scholars approached the problem with the tools of analysis of the social scientist and/or social historian, although it is true that some of them were more interested in the social characteristics of the military than they were in the structure of the society in which professional soldiers operated. Secondly, there was a considerable reluctance in the 1960s to use the term 'militarism' with reference to developing countries. American political scientists and sociologists in particular preferred to speak of civil-military relations. This tendency was very marked among non-Marxist social scientists, just as they were wary of such politically charged expressions as 'backwardness' and 'underdeveloped' when they wrote about Third World countries. However, this should not deter us from using the concept of militarism now, if we are talking about historically comparable phenomena and if it helps us to clarify the issues.

Thirdly, there was an early phase in the debate when it was considered more desirable to develop classificatory schemes which would make it possible to put each of the 'New Nations' (Morris Janowitz) into a box within a 'grid' of clearly defined characteristics. Thus, the British political scientists Samuel E. Finer, in his famous study of 1962,[4] examined the importance of the 'level of political culture' as well as the societal milieu in which the military operated and proposed to distinguish four stages: 'minimal political culture', 'low political culture', 'developed political culture' and 'mature political culture'. Finer's underlying conceptual framework is not difficult to grasp, if one knows that he would accord the Western democracies the status of 'mature political culture' and that he believed the intervention of the military in politics to be more likely in countries where the political institutions are weak and lacking in legitimacy. Ten years later, Robin Luckham of Sussex University constructed a 'grid' which, he claimed, removed some of the deficiencies of the schemes provided by Finer and others.[5] He tried to relate several variables to each other, i.e. the respective strengths of military and civilian institutions, the interaction between the two spheres and the degree to which the military 'boundaries' are open to penetration from the outside. The result was the following 'grid' which was supposed to be capable of accommodating all types of countries:[6]

Civil Power	Military Power	Boundaries		
		Integral	Fragmented	Permeated
High	High	a Objective Control	c Apparat Control	
High	Medium	b Constabulary Control	d Nation-in-Arms	
High	Low		e Revolutionary Nation-in-Arms	f Subjective Control
Not High	High	g Garrison State		
Not High	Medium	h Guardian State		
Not High	Medium	i Post-Colonial Guardian State		
Not High	Low	l Political Vacuum		

a) Western Europe and North America.
b) E.g. present-day Japan, Ireland, Sweden.
c) E.g. USSR, Nazi Germany, Fascist Italy, China, Yugoslavia.
d) E.g. Israel.
e) E.g. Cuba, Vietnam, Algeria.
f) Traditional societies of Africa or eighteenth-century Europe.

g) Very similar to Lasswell's original conception.
h) E.g. Egypt in 1952, Ghana in 1966.
i) E.g. Mali 1968.
k) E.g. Latin American, Middle East.
l) Congo prior to Mobutu.

Much of the optimism of the 1960s has evaporated by now and few scholars would be as courageous as the American political scientist Amos Perlmutter who believed that it would be possible to agree on a few key variables and to develop a list of criteria against which any given country could be checked.[7] In the past ten years, most experts have concentrated on specific cases so that there is now a fairly extensive literature on Third World countries as far apart geographically as Brazil, Nigeria, Iraq and Thailand.

Yet, despite the proliferation of meticulous and valuable monographic research in the 1970s, implicitly or explicitly one major problem has remained a key issue among social scientists, i.e. whether or not the military in developing countries are a 'modernizing' force. In 1962, Finer had no solution to this question. He merely offered a static model of levels of 'political culture', without saying how the transition to a higher level might be achieved. However, only a few years later there emerged a growing number of scholars who argued that Third World armies must ultimately be analysed in the light of the problem of modernization. It will be immediately obvious that this question is in fact a very old one, if one looks at the history of the debate on militarism. But it was dressed up in new clothes by the military sociologists. One of them was Lucien Pye whose article on 'Armies in the Process of Political Modernization' appeared in 1968.[8]

Pye started from the hypothesis that the attempt to establish modern institutions and organizations in 'traditional' societies in the Third World had been most successful in the military field. The military organizations of these countries had been taken from the developed societies and thus represented to Pye in many ways almost an 'ideal-type industrial and secularized enterprise'. Similarly, he continued, the officer corps was selected according to principles which were very different from those of the surrounding 'traditional' society. What is more: 'The revolution in military technology has caused the army leaders of the newly emergent societies to be extremely sensitive to the extent to which their countries are economically and technologically underdeveloped. Called upon roles basic to advanced societies, the more politically conscious officers can hardly avoid being aware of the need for substantial changes in their own societies.'

This observation led Pye to ask what role armies might play 'in shaping the attitudes toward modernity in other spheres of society'. That this question had not been raised before was, according to Pye, due to the ideological preconceptions of the Anglo-Saxon social sciences and in particular to the Western stereotype of the military as 'a foe of liberal values'. He tried to leave this tradition behind him by arguing that the army was 'one of the more modernized of the authoritative agencies in transitional societies'. He therefore exhorted the West to develop 'effective relationships' with the military in developing countries. Third World armies, he believed, are best equipped to initiate and channel social and political change. Military aid is hence most valuable development aid. Pye was not the only scholar to propound this view. Writing on the role of the military in South-East Asia, his colleague Guy Pauker came to the conclusion that officers in that part of the world were not 'the product of social classes with feudal traditions'.[9] Because of their own social background and their historical experiences they could also hardly be considered 'the natural allies of feudal or other vested interests'. On the contrary, Pauker concluded, 'their natural propensities' were 'progressive'.

It is obvious that this was indeed a new departure, if one remembers the traditional Western critique of the military as discussed in earlier chapters. On the other hand, it would be a mistake to view Pye's explicit appeal to abandon Anglo-Saxon suspicions of the military as a complete rejection of the older anti-militarist critique. His concern with Third World modernization must be seen in the broader context of evolutionary theories of society. It is hardly conceivable that he wished the Third World to take any other road than that leading towards a capitalist-industrial society. Yet, unlike Spencer, he did not see this as a quasi-automatic development. This was after all the period of the Cold War and of competition with Marxist models, whether of the Soviet or the Maoist variety. At the same time the terms 'Westernization' or 'Europeanization' had an ominous ring to the ears of the inhabitants of former colonial countries. 'Modernization' was clearly a more neutral concept; but behind it stood the ideal of American institutions to be held up to others for copying. The assumption that economic growth generated by a free-market economy would further the creation of viable parliamentary-democratic institutions and that such institutions would in turn be stabilized by industrialization along Western lines had become a widely accepted credo among American social scientists. Famous sociologists like Seymour Lipset were among its advocates, and Talcott Parsons spent many years trying to provide an answer to the question of the conditions under which this Western system had developed.[10] Walt Rostow produced his well-known *Stages of Economic Growth* which, significantly enough, he sub-titled 'A Non-Communist Manifesto'.[11]

There is no need to go into the details of this general discussion of the preconditions of growth and the origins of Western institutions. The point is that certain notions concerning the evolution of industrial capitalism and liberal parliamentarism had become deeply ingrained in Western political and economic thought. At the same time, this self-image of the West cannot be understood without the perception of a threat by the Second World and without reference to an implicit or explicit concern for the future of the Third. This is also the broader context in which Pye's work has to be seen; for he was prominent in a group of scholars who gathered in the Committee on Comparative Politics and who tried to construct a system of categories with the help of which they hoped to make the whole problem of economic and political development intelligible. Since the sociology of organization and structure of institutions was one of their starting points, it is not surprising that they became interested in the military in Third World countries. Could it be that they were vital pacemakers in the process of 'modernization'? And if so, maybe it was time to abandon the long-standing suspicion of the military, at least when the 'New Nations' — rather than Prussia or nineteenth-century Japan — were being analysed? Yet was the militarism of transitional societies really a 'progressive' force? This question was bound to provide a good deal of controversy. It is interesting that this debate coincided with a renewed discussion of the nature of National Socialism as a phenomenon typical of the transnational societies of Central Europe some thirty years earlier. Here it was especially the German sociologist Ralf Dahrendorf and later the American historian David Schoenbaum who advanced the hypothesis that Hitler's warrior regime had dragged Germany into the twentieth century and had laid, inadvertently perhaps, the foundations of the modern socio-economic structures upon which the high-technology industrialism and the liberal parliamentarism of the Federal Republic could be built after 1945.[12]

To be sure, just as Dahrendorf's and Schoenbaum's arguments were disputed, doubt was soon also cast upon the work of the Committee on Comparative Politics. Early grumbles of dissatisfaction could be heard from the Chicago sociologist Morris Janowitz in his book *The Military in the Political Development of New Nations*.[13] In his first chapter, Janowitz asked a number of questions which it is worth repeating at this point because they are indicative of the kind of problems with which the experts were preoccupied at a time when the position of the army in developing countries and the role of the military in political change were on the agenda. The first of these questions was: 'What characteristics of the military establishment of a new nation facilitate its involvement in domestic politics?' The other problem was 'what are the capabilities of the military to supply effective political leadership for a new nation striving for rapid economic development and social modernization?'

The answers to these questions, Janowitz continued, were in many ways 'very similar'. For

> those organizational and professional qualities which make it possible for the military of a new nation to accumulate political power, and even to take over political power, are the same as those which limit its ability to rule effectively. Thus once political power has been achieved, the military must develop mass political organizations of a civilian type, or it must work out viable relations with civilian political groups.

Put differently, it is 'relatively easy for the military to seize power in a new nation', but 'it is much more difficult for it to govern'. These statements led him to ask two further questions, namely 'why are military officers of new nations, as compared with those in Western industrialized societies, more influential in domestic politics?' Secondly, why does the capacity of the military to act in politics differ from country to country? As to the first question, Janowitz had no doubt that it was the 'social structure of their countries' which predisposed them to 'political activism'. The answer to the second question, he felt, was more dependent upon the 'characteristics of the military profession' in the nations concerned. It seems fair to say that Janowitz, in the final analysis, would wish to attach as much weight to societal forces defining the position of the military as he would give to military influence on politics, even if in 1964 he showed a slight analytical preference for the latter. If, he concluded, one aims to 'give more concrete meaning to the forms of militarism in the new nations', the task would be to clarify the contribution made by the professional military to 'different patterns of domestic politics'.

It is easy to make too much of this statement and of the opposite position which Samuel Huntington took up in 1968.[14] As Finer has pointed out, 'Huntington was as sensitive to the importance of social and organizational characteristics of the military as Janowitz was to those of the society',[15] and it may even be that the latter has been misunderstood. Nevertheless, these were the two names around whom the debate on civil-military relations in Third World countries and different forms of militarism developed in the 1960s. It seems best to

introduce it here by reference to Janowitz. Before expounding his own
view of the relationship between social structure and military organization, he dealt with, and ultimately discarded, a number of alternative
approaches to the analysis of the military in the Third World. Thus he
wondered if any yardsticks could be gained by means of certain quantitative factors, such as the size of a particular country, of its army or of
its population, but doubted this in the end. Nor did he think that the
history of a former colony, the historical roots of the army in question
and the time-span that had elapsed since independence would provide
reliable guides for comparisons and systematization. Finally, he also
dismissed the attempt to correlate economic growth with the role of
the military in politics. In particular, he was critical of Lipset who had
used certain indices of economic development to compare a number of
Latin American and Western European countries. He applied the
same criticism to James Coleman's comparative work on selected
nations in Asia, the Middle East and Africa. Janowitz concluded that
Coleman's 'type of analysis appears to have limited relevance for
understanding, on a comparative basis, the dynamic relationship
between economic development and political forms'.[16]

His next step was to caution against a view of modernization, held
by members of the Committee on Comparative Politics, which saw
'traditional' societies as unchanging entities before the 'introduction of
modern technology, modern administration and Western values'. This
view, he insisted, 'is a continuation of the "idea of progress" in a
non-Western context'. On the contrary, 'peasant societies undergo
change, including rapid and drastic change, on occasion, as peasant
technology changes. In particular, as peasant societies, new nations
were touched by colonialism in the past, and some were completely
transformed by colonial agricultural and plantation systems.' He
added that since religious values were paramount in this kind of
society, 'an understanding of the sociological implications of traditional religion is essential for understanding the structure of these
societies'. One such structural feature which was central was that 'the
organization of a peasant society rests in the linkage between vast
masses of rural population and tiny urban elites who manage the
societal institutions'.

It is now easier to see why Janowitz's approach to the problem of
modernization had important implications for the role assigned to the
military in 'traditional' societies. There exists, he continued, a widespread notion of the military being 'technocratic in orientation' and
'concerned with modernization'. Such a view — and we have discussed
it above — ignored the fact that 'the military is also concerned with

legitimate authority and with historical and national traditions'. In view of this it would be downright dangerous to 'overlook the impact of neo-traditionalism on the military'. The most he is therefore prepared to concede is that 'the military operate at each level of political intervention, including the takeover of political power, as incomplete agents of political change'. This conclusion, which was evidently at variance with Pye's and Pauker's, was supported by the findings of Victor Alba when he analysed 'The Stages of Militarism in Latin America'.[17] The objectives of the military in that part of the world, he asserted, were, 'except for Perón and others of his kind,. . . generally more of a police than a reformist nature'.[18] This was also the view of Edwin Lieuwen who saw Latin American militarism as a political force 'that, on balance, brings social change and reform programs to a halt'.[19]

There is also Irving Horowitz's verdict that without the military, 'nearly every Latin American republic would stand politically to the left of where it now is'.[20] To Martin Needler, finally, it was quite clear 'that, if one has to generalize about the role of the Latin American military as a whole, one must consider their role, on balance, still to be a conservative or reactionary one'.[21]

Yet these conclusions were not necessarily believed to have universal applicability. Alba at least apparently wished to see them confined to Latin America and would presumably have agreed with Manfred Halpern's findings on the military in Middle Eastern politics whom Halpern saw as 'the vanguard of nationalism and social reform',[22] However, this notion did not go unchallenged either. In 1970 Eric Nordlinger published the most categorical rebuttal of the Pye-Halpern position.[23] He found 'that, except under certain conditions, soldiers in mufti are not agents of modernization'. It was, he added, not just in Latin America, but also in the Middle East, in North Africa and in Asia that 'officer-politicians either fail to contribute to economic change or oppose modernizing demands and efforts where these exist'. The occasional use of revolutionary language by officers in the Third World should not lead one to think otherwise. For in most cases he had found their slogans to be empty rhetoric:

> By stating their cause in terms of modernization and reform, middle-level officers can oppose and then replace their conservative superiors. Once having installed themselves in power, some of these officers will act in accordance with their original goals. On the other hand, this reasoning also suggests why so many of the young officers who apparently begin their political adventures as ardent reformers become conservatives only a few

short months after their *coups*. They were not convinced re-
formers to begin with; they simply used the call for economic and
social change for the realization of their own class and status
interests.

It was, of course, one thing to state that the military in developing
countries did not fulfil a modernizing role, but quite another to put
forward plausible explanations of this. In this connection we must now
take a closer look at Huntington's work. His contribution is important
for three interrelated reasons. Firstly, even if we accept Finer's con-
ciliatory remark that Huntington and Janowitz are not that far apart,
the fact remains that Huntington has stated quite unceremoniously
that it would be 'fallacious to attempt to explain military interventions
in politics primarily by reference to the internal structure of the
military or the social background of the officers doing the intervening'.[24] Although he admits that there is some evidence to support
the kind of connections which Janowitz is presumed to have drawn,
there is also contradicting evidence. Consequently, 'the effort to
answer the question "What characteristics of the military establishment of a new nation facilitate its involvement in domestic politics?" is
misdirected because the most important causes of military intervention
in politics are not military, but political and reflect not the social and
organizational characteristics of the military establishment, but the
political and institutional structure of society'.[25]

This social-structural approach implied, secondly, that Huntington
was not interested in restricting the modernization argument to certain
continents. His test was, so to speak, a sociological one and hence
applicable anywhere in the world. The third peculiarity of Huntington's analysis is his basic pessimism. Although he, too, operated within
the broad framework of modernization theory and saw military intervention in politics as a 'striking' aspect of it, he did not see Third World
development as an evolution towards a better state of affairs. Rather
he puts forward an interpretation of 'political decay' which leads him
to take up a politically conservative position. What then is the process
affecting underdeveloped societies which Huntington tries to tackle
with the tools of a sociologist?

He starts from the basic assumption that 'the general politicization
of social forces and institutions' is the most important feature of
all developing societies. He called this type of politicized society
'praetorian' on the understanding 'that this refers to the participation
not only of the military, but of other social forces as well'. Thus trade
unions, businessmen, students and religious organizations may all be
involved in politics. However, what is special about the praetorian

society is 'the absence of effective political institutions capable of mediating, refining and moderating group political action'. The big question was therefore whether praetorian societies would be able to develop such institutions, and on this point the choice was a straightforward one. If they succeeded, a 'civic society' would emerge, by which he presumably meant a Western-type political system. If, on the other hand, they failed, 'the result of social and economic modernization is political chaos' and revolution.

However, before either state was reached, praetorianism would pass through a number of phases. The first — 'oligarchical' — phase was dominated by three social forces: 'The great landowners, the leading clergy and the wielders of the sword'. But their time would eventually come to an end as 'almost all praetorian oligarchies. . . evolve into radical praetorian systems'. Huntington saw the key to this second phase in the entry of middle-class groups into politics. Political participation widened and finally led to radical praetorianism. For, 'the middle-class makes its debut on the political scene not in the frock of the merchant, but in the epaulettes of the colonel'. Increasingly the officers are themselves drawn from middle-class background. They acquire a 'distinctive character and esprit' and become receptive not only to nationalism, but also to ideas of progress. Ultimately 'the officers and their civilian allies form themselves into cliques and secret societies to discuss the future of their nation and to plot the overthrow of its rulers', and one day they will succeed.

Apart from helping to destroy oligarchical praetorianism, 'the military officers play [another and] highly modernizing and progressive role' in that

> they promote social and economic reform, national integration and, in some measure, the extension, of political participation. They assail waste, backwardness and corruption, and they introduce into the society highly middle-class ideas of efficiency, honesty and national loyalty. Like the Protestant entrepreneurs of western Europe, the soldier reformers in non-Western societies embody and promote a puritanism which, while not as extreme perhaps as that of the radical revolutionaries, is nonetheless a distinctive innovation in their societies.

Thus the revolt against oligarchical praetorianism at the same time clears 'the way for the entry of other middle-class elements into politics'. However, according to Huntington, this is not the final stage in the process of modernization in praetorian societies. The broadening of political participation which had ushered in the radical phase continues and with it begins the political mobilization of the lower classes. At this point the radical and progressive role of the soldier undergoes an important change: 'As the mass society looms on the horizon, he becomes the conservative guardian of the existing order'. And if by this time no effective political institutions have been developed, the military, Huntington concluded, would find themselves 'engaged in a conservative effort to protect the existing system against the incursion of the lower classes, particularly the urban lower classes'.

Armies thus assume the role of 'door-keepers in the expansion of political participation in a praetorian society'. Having opened the gates to the middle-class, they now act to lock it on the lower class. Seen in historical perspective, 'the radical phase of a praetorian society begins with a bright modernizing military coup toppling the oligarchy and heralding the emergence of enlightenment into politics. It ends in a succession of frustrating and unwholesome rearguard efforts to block the lower classes from scaling the heights of political power.' During the phase of mass praetorianism, coups therefore gain the function of 'veto interventions' which take place either when the military wish to block 'the actual or prospective victory at the polls of a party or movement' which they dislike and wish to see excluded from political power or when 'a government in power begins to promote radical policies or to develop an appeal to groups' which are politically unacceptable to the military.

It is these developments during the transition from radical to mass praetorianism which inspire Huntington's pessimism concerning the continued viability of these societies. He believes that the promotion of social and economic reform will be tendentially incompatible with the concomitant expansion of political participation and that both together will exert a destabilizing influence on these societies, unless effective political institutions can be built. Without such institutions, the modernization process, as perceived by Huntington, will ultimately plunge praetorian countries into anarchy and prevent the emergence of a 'civic society'. In view of this, much depends on how far it will be possible to create, during the phase of radical praetorianism, conditions of stability in which the military can operate as 'institution-builders'. According to Huntington, conditions of stability are most likely to obtain where the military succeed either in forging a coalition with the middle-class intelligentsia against the mass of the rural population or in coalescing with the peasants against '[the] brains'. The third alternative, the alliance between the intelligentsia and the rural masses, he asserts, 'usually' involves revolution, and this is precisely what he dreads. Considering that the first alternative ('guns and brains') is very rare, a 'guns-and-numbers' coalition appears to be the most promising from Huntington's point of view. Yet he displays a marked reluctance to rate its chances of success very highly. What militates against success is that 'the distinctive aspect of radical praetorianism is the divorce of the city from the countryside'. Politics in effect takes place as a struggle among the urban middle-class groups, whereas the 'social precondition for the establishment of stability' is the reappearance in politics of the social forces dominant in the countryside.

Will the military be able to bridge the gap between town and country with its destabilizing consequences? Huntington is inclined to doubt it because 'the military are locked in a middle-class outlook'. They are hence unlikely to take a broader perspective which would enable them to construct the kind of coalitional basis from which 'institution-building' might successfully proceed. Moreover, the soldier's subjective attitude towards modern politics and towards parties will lead him to 'shrink from assuming the role of a political organizer'. In short, the prospects of praetorianism avoiding political chaos are slim. This verdict did not prevent Huntington from ending with what amounts to an appeal:

> In many societies the opportunity the military have for political creativity may be the last real chance for political institutionalization short of the totalitarian road. If the military fail to seize that opportunity, the broadening of participation transforms the society into a mass praetorian system. In such a system the opportunity to create political institutions passes from the military, the apostles of order, to those other middle-class leaders who are the apostles of revolution.

Huntington had no time for the latter.

The Marxists were, of course, also among those particularly interested in the connection between the military and the social and political structures of Third World countries. Nor is it surprising that they were bound to disagree with scholars like Huntington on central points, most of all the need for revolutionary upheaval. But before these differences will be illustrated, it is worth emphasizing the considerable area agreement which had come to exist between Marxist and non-Marxist social scientists and which will be further examined in a broader context below.[26] After all, there were quite a few writers who refused to ascribe a progressive function to the military in Third World countries. Huntington was at least prepared to concede that armies would be strongholds of conservatism and reaction under *mass* praetorianism. More than that: his approach and in particular his analysis of the middle-class resembled in many ways the Marxist interpretation of the bourgeoisie during the period of its rise and subsequent decline. His terminology, to be sure, was different, but his underlying view of societal evolution much less so.

On the other hand, disagreement persisted mainly in two areas. Firstly, Marxists found it very difficult to assign to the military a post-independence progressiveness in the way Huntington had done. Secondly, they were critical of the virtual absence in non-Marxist writings of any attempt to incorporate the international dimension into the analysis. To them industrial capitalism was a global system, and any model which tended to treat the Third World and its armed forces as operating in an international vacuum was, for this reason alone, regarded as unsatisfactory. Of course, 'the armies and class structures of the peripheral countries' were not just seen as having become 'those of the advanced countries writ small'.[27] But they had certainly been 'profoundly distorted by their contact with the latter', and permanently so. Furthermore, 'the techniques and organizational blueprints of advanced countries are transferred to the Third World, interlinked with arms sales and industrialisation'.[28]

One of those scholars who took a pronounced stand against the 'modernization school' was the Marxist sociologist Bassam Tibi whose book on the subject of militarism in the Third World appeared in 1973.[29] Although he had harsh words for Pye and Huntington, Tibi would not consider all Third World armies reactionary. To begin with, he drew a distinction between 'armies in Europe which are marked by an aristocratic, militaristic tradition and armies of underdeveloped countries'. Secondly, there existed, he believed, 'historical situations in which [Third World] armies acted in fact as a progressive force'. These situations arose in the period prior to liberation from colonial rule. Tibi, in other words, proposed to make the achievement of independence the watershed beyond which the military began to play a conservative role.

In this connection he attached, as one might expect, considerable importance to the 'national revolutionary petty bourgeoisie' which had been produced by the colonial economy prior to independence. This social group was to play a progressive role during the liberation struggle, and as the officer corps of the countries concerned had been largely recruited from the petty bourgeoisie, they, too, were a progressive element by acting as the 'extended mailed fist' of the former. However, according to Tibi, the function of the military changed as soon as independence had been won. The army and the social groups in which it was rooted now became concerned to safeguard their own position and were hence prone to enter into alliances with pre-independence oligarchies. The soldiers turned into a factor, powerful by virtue of their command of the means of physical violence, which hindered the post-liberation transformation of the country's economic structures as well as the emancipation of the masses. Tibi finally dealt with the assumption that Third World officer corps were integrated into what he called the 'international militaristic system' which reinforced the military's preoccupation with order and stability. All these factors taken together would, of course, work in favour of a rigid status quo preservation and, ultimately, the emergence of a military dictatorship. And in the long run they would also work to create a revolutionary situation from which a socialist system would be born.

We are thus once again left with the familiar difference between the frameworks in which Marxists and non-Marxists have tended to interpret civil-military relations since the nineteenth century. Nevertheless, this should not blind us to the considerable measure of agreement which had grown up between analysts like Huntington, on the one hand, and Tibi, on the other. Certainly their categories and methodology are quite different from those which dominated the debate concerning Prusso-German militarism. They are clearly sociological and, as far as Huntington and Tibi are concerned, focus on socioeconomic structures. At the same time there is a good deal of consensus between Tibi and those who propose to approach the problem through the organizational and institutional peculiarities of Third World armies. Tibi, too, operates with the notion that military organizations are often 'enclaves' within underdeveloped societies. The result of this is that 'authority problems. . . arise not only between high-ranking officers in command positions and young officers with [advanced] technical skills, but also between the army as a whole, representing a social institution with modern, technically and rationally functioning structures', on the one hand, and the rule of the older agrarian and bureaucratic oligarchies, on the other. Such authority problems, Tibi concluded, may well provide a further impetus for the military to interfere with the social and economic development of a particular country in a 'progressive' direction. Huntington would presumably not have found this conclusion objectionable.

A shift of emphasis has finally also taken place with reference to the question of the 'external dependence' of Third World countries. The volume by Philippe C. Schmitter, which has already been mentioned in another context,[30] is a good example of the growing interest by non-Marxist social scientists in the hegemonic role of the superpowers and in particular of the 'United States in the Western Hemisphere.' The book contains, for example, an article by James R. Kurth on the 'United States Foreign Policy and Latin American Military Rule' which tries to take account of Marxist writings on the 'development of underdevelopment'[31] and the implications of the Vietnam experience.[32] His conclusions are certainly highly critical of U.S. foreign policy in general and of military aid programmes and their effect upon Latin American development in particular,[33] although he does not regard this aspect of superpower politics as deserving of the label 'militaristic'.

Marxist analysts, on the other hand, have been less cautious in this respect. They have tended to see the military involvement of the metropolitan countries in Third World areas as one component of a 'militarism' of the advanced industrial nations. There is hence not merely a debate on militarism with reference to the problem of 'back-wardness' and 'modernization' in developing countries, but also one relating to the role of the military in the United States, Western Europe and the Soviet Union. It is to this controversy, which has ancient roots, but which came to revolve around a new concept — the 'Military Industrial Complex' — that we must now turn.

Notes

1   See also below pp. 111ff.
2   W. Sauer, 'Die politische Geschichte der deutschen Armee und das Problem des Militarismus.' *Politische Vierteljahresschrift* 5 (1965), p. 350.
3   The divergence from Hintze and Herzfeld who had attached some importance to geographical position (insular vs. continental) could not be more marked. See above pp. 14 and 8 .
4   S.E. Finer, *The Man on Horseback*, London 1962.
5   A.R. Luckham, 'A Comparative Typology of Civil-Military Relations'. *Government and Opposition* 6 (1971), pp. 5-35.
6   Ibid., p.22.
7   A. Perlmutter, *The Military and Politics in Modern Times*, New Haven 1977. On recent trends see also S.E. Finer, 'The Statesmanship of Arms.' *Times Literary Supplement*, 17.2.1978, p.217.
8   In J.J. Johnson, ed., *The Role of the Military in Underdeveloped Countries*, Princeton 1968, pp. 69ff.
9   G. Pauker, 'Southeast Asia as a Problem Area in the Next Decade.' *World Politics* 11 (1959), pp. 339ff.
10   S.M. Lipset, *Political Man,* London 1960; T. Parsons, *The Social System,* London 1951.
11   W.W. Rostow, *The Stages of Economic Growth*, Cambridge (Mass.) 1960.
12   R. Dahrendorf, *Gesellschaft und Demokratie in Deutschland*, München 1968; D. Schoenbaum, *Hitler's Social Revolution*, London 1967.
13   M. Janowitz, *The Military in the Political Development of New Nations*, Chicago 1964, esp. pp.1ff.
14   S.P. Huntington, *Political Order in Changing Societies*. New Haven 1968.

15 S.E. Finer, 'The Statesmanship of Arms', p.217.

16 M. Janowitz, *The Military in the Political Development*, p.19.

17 In J.J. Johnson ed., *The Role of the Military*, pp. 165-80.

18 Ibid., p.179.

19 E. Lieuwen, *Generals vs. Presidents. Neo-Militarism in Latin America*, London 1964, p. 135.

20 I.L. Horowitz, 'The Military Elites', in S.M. Lipset and A. Solari, eds., *Elites in Latin America*, London 1967, p. 147.

21 M.C. Needler, *The United States and the Latin American Revolution*, Boston 1972, p.45. A cross-reference must be made at this point to a volume by P.C. Schmitter, ed., *Military Rule in Latin America*, Beverly Hills-London 1973, which contains essays by Alain Rouquié, Jerry L. Weaver, Geoffrey Kemp, James R. Kurth and Schmitter himself and which takes issue with the generalizations by Needler and others. If one follows Schmitter's introductory remarks (ibid., p. VIII), Rouquié and Weaver would seem to overturn the above-mentioned statements. However, a close reading of both contributions reveals that the editor apparently got carried away by what he believed to be the '*substantive originality*' and '*critical perspective*' (ibid., Schmitter's emphasis) of his book. Having studied the Bolivian and Peruvian cases, Rouquié would still not wish to disagree with other authors that well into the 1960s the military in both countries were not a force of reform and revolution. He tries to show that a new phase began in the late 1960s, but then adds so many caveats to his conclusion that it hardly amounts to a resurrection of the arguments by Pye and Pauker. Weaver, while raising important points about the *cui bono* of military intervention and military rule in Latin America, likewise appears to be aiming for a 'substantial refinement' of received views rather than their recasting. The authors make two further points, one of which is of significance here: they try to differentiate between the intentional policies of the military regimes of Latin America and the often unintended consequences of these policies as regards structural change. This is clearly a valid differentiation. In the long-run, conservative policies have often had surprising 'revolutionary' consequences. Bismarck's introduction of universal manhood suffrage in 1867/71 is a particularly striking example. On the second substantive point raised by Schmitter's volume, see below pp. 81f.

22 M. Halpern, *The Politics of Social Change in the Middle East and North Africa*, Princeton 1963, p.75.

23 E.A. Nordlinger, 'Soldiers in Mufti. The Impact of Military Rule on Economic and Social Change in the Non-Western States.' *American Political Science Review* 66 (1970), pp. 1131ff. See also his recent book *Soldiers in Politics*, Englewood Cliffs 1977.

24 S.P. Huntington, *Political Order*, p.193.

25 Ibid., p.194.

26 See below pp. 106ff.

27 A.R. Luckham, 'Militarism: Force, Class and International Conflict.' *IDS-Bulletin* (July 1977), p.23. On Luckham's earlier, non-Marxist position see above p. 69.

28 Ibid.

29 B. Tibi, *Militär und Sozialismus in der Dritten Welt*, Frankfurt 1973, esp. Chapter 1 for the following. For another Marxist critique of Pye, see A.R. Luckham, 'The Military, Militarism and Dependence in the Third World. A

Theoretical Sketch', in C.N. Enloe and U. Semin-Panzer, eds., *The Military, the Police and Domestic Order,* London 1976, p.172. For an East German assessment of the problem, see M. Kossok, 'Changes in the Political and Social Function of the Armed Forces in Developing Countries', in M. Janowitz and J. van Doorn, eds., *On Military Intervention,* Rotterdam 1971, pp.405-24.

30   See above, p. 83, note 21.
31   A.G. Frank, *Latin America: Underdevelopment or Revolution. Essays on the Development of Underdevelopment and the Immediate Enemy,* New York-London 1969.
32   J.R. Kurth, 'United States Foreign Policy and Latin American Military Rule', in P.C. Schmitter, ed., *Military Rule in Latin America,* pp.244-322.
33   Ibid., p. 314.

V The Military-Industrial Complex

It has emerged from the previous two chapters that the views of Marxist and non-Marxist writers on the problem of civil-military relations in developing societies have converged in recent years to a degree which it would have been difficult to conceive of a generation ago. This applies both to the interpretative framework in which the cases of Germany and Japan are now being considered and to the phenomenon of militarism in the Third World. We are now left with the question of whether changes of position can also be discerned with reference to the debate on militarism in developed industrial societies.

Turning to the Marxist position first, it becomes clear that little change has taken place on the question of principle: capitalist-industrial societies are still by definition militaristic. In this respect the official Soviet attitude differs little from that of the neo-Marxists in the West. Many non-Marxist scholars, on the other hand, will deny that the term is applicable to Western industrial societies while pointing to various manifestations of a 'Soviet militarism'. Both sides presented their respective arguments with considerable vigour in the 1950s, with the East-West confrontation obviously providing the wider political backdrop. The other noteworthy feature of the debate on militarism during the Cold War period is that its participants from the West tended to employ a yardstick which had figured in the older Anglo-Saxon discussion: militarism was said to be in evidence where civilian decision-making was excessively influenced by the military and by military considerations.

Seen from this perspective, the Western case seemed clear-cut: it was wrong to talk of militarism where there existed large, well-organized private associations, agreed procedures for the transfer of power and legitimated governments. Strong civilian institutions were seen to guarantee civilian control of political decision-making, including that concerning military affairs. In short, Western parliamentary democracies could not be called militaristic. However, when these criteria were applied to the Soviet case, the result was deemed to be very different and it was justified to speak of a 'Soviet militarism'.

Nevertheless, although the case may seem to be a powerful one, a number of well-known authorities have always been hesitant to apply the term to socialist countries. One of these sceptics is John Erickson, one of the foremost experts on Soviet military affairs. Taking another look at the problem in 1971, he doubted that even Stalin's Russia could be called militaristic.[1]* For, 'although military requirements and assumptions influenced political decisions to a considerable degree and were at times even decisive', the predominance of the Communist Party of the Soviet Union (CPSU) had always been assured. Civilian control of the military, in other words, had never been in doubt.

If Erickson's points had been generally accepted, the whole debate on militarism might have come to a conclusion at this point. The term would be considered applicable to historical cases such as those of Prussia-Germany or Japan or, alternatively, to certain types of regimes in the Third World in our period. However, it was not merely Marxist writers who, with their particular view of capitalist societies, refused to let the problem rest there. There was also a growing number of non-Marxist analysts who probed further and in particular those among them who, as we have seen, had become increasingly interested in socio-economic questions. More specifically, they had begun to wonder whether the traditional distinction between civilianism and militarism was still a useful one where present-day America and Russia were concerned.

In 1961, this discussion received a major boost by a man who could be assumed to know what he was talking about: Dwight D. Eisenhower, ex-general and retiring President of the United States. In his Farewell Address in January of that year, he warned the American nation of the 'conjunction of an immense military establishment and a large arms industry'.[2] The United States, he added, 'must guard against the acquisition of unwarranted influence, whether sought or unsought, by the military-industrial complex. The potential for the disastrous rise of misplaced power exists and will persist'.

Eisenhower's concept of a Military-Industrial Complex (MIC) has since then aroused much academic controversy and produced plenty of empirical research into its various components.[3] Apart from bringing together much interesting statistical material on the operations of the American armaments industry and the politics of the Pentagon bureaucracy, one result of this work has been that the sociological and institutional scope within which the Complex is being examined has been extended very considerably. Initially the MIC had been conceived of as a coalition between the armed forces and the arms manufacturers for the purpose, not of waging war, but of maintaining large military expenditures. But soon attention of researchers also turned to the educational system, the research institutes, the trade unions and to Congressional leaders representing regions in which important sections of the electorate were employed by the military supply industries. The underlying hypothesis was that the objective of the military-industrial alliance could not be secured over a longer time-span unless other factors were won over to, and included in, the original coalition. Scholars like the Bremen University political scientist Dieter Senghaas would consider this interpretation of institutions to have been successful and hence speak of a 'political - ideological - military - scientific - technological - industrial' complex.[4]

This semantic monster makes a crucial point relating to the debate on militarism to which the American historian Vernon K. Dibble gave succinct expression some years ago.[5] He argued that it is 'meaningless' to ask whether or not the civilians control the military. In his view, the United States had become a country in which institutions and men who possessed military, economic and political power had become so dependent upon each other that the military and civilian spheres had merged into one inseparable whole or, at least, had entered into a symbiotic relationship. The interests and objectives of the elites and of the institutions dominated by them had become so complementary that the traditional argument concerning the relationship between civilians and soldiers in industrial societies was no longer applicable. Extending C. Wright Mills's analysis of the American 'power elite',[6] Dibble believed that the United States had become a 'garrison society'. This concept was, of course, derived from Lasswell's term ('Garrison State'), but Dibble insisted that Lasswell's approach had placed the 'specialists on violence' at the centre. Dibble, on the other hand, laid the stress on the coalitional aspect of certain groups within the 'garrison society'. As regards the question of whether this coalition operated in competition against other interest formations in the sense of a pluralist society or whether it formed 'an omnipotent elite committed to militarism'[7], he, like Mills, came down on the side of the latter view.

Still, the problem remained as to whether this type of society can be called militaristic. Senghaas and a number of other authors have said so, but added that the term's traditional meaning should be enlarged.[8] However, looking at the kind of issues that are being debated among scholars of the Military-Industrial Complex, it seems more sensible to speak of an altogether different type of militarism. After all, the starting point of MIC research is different in the sense that it focuses on high-technology industrial countries, in particular America and Russia, engaged in a modern arms race. The salient feature of this military competition is that it is about very sophisticated weapons which are quickly becoming obsolete and are constantly being replaced by the next 'generation' of even more sophisticated war materials.

We are, in other words, dealing with arms races in the nuclear and missile age which required a 'sustained deployment of research, military technology and industrial capabilities which, in view of the continuous cost increases of research, development, production and installation of technologically advanced weapons systems, not only swallow up enormous sums of money and tie up resources, but. . . also program the development process of the countries concerned.'[9] It is not difficult to see how this turns into a spiral without end and how technological innovation can become a dynamic factor in its own right. However, analysts have been cautious not to reduce the whole problem of the MIC to the pressures of rapid technological change and to ignore human action and socio-economic forces. And in taking an interest in these factors, non-Marxists saw the methodological gap between themselves and Marxist writers, who, since Luxemburg, had been interested in the political economy of modern arms races, narrowing. At least the debate is conducted on the same terrain.

Yet, real differences remain and this is the place to examine some of them. Thus the non-Marxists have tended to disagree that the representatives of the MIC coalition promote the arms race in a cynical frame of mind. Instead they are seen as captives of an ideology of conflict and national security which originated in the Cold War period. It is the fear of finding oneself on the losing side and of becoming exposed to political pressure which has resulted in an almost obsessive preoccupation with the concept of deterrence. It is argued that the peculiar perceptions of the East-West conflict provide a much more powerful stimulus to the arms race than technological innovation. Senghaas has even gone so far as to describe the state of mind in which the managers of the MIC find themselves as 'autistic'.[10] He means by this that their perceptions of reality have become so distorted by suspicion and fear that little or no attention is being paid to the opponent's actual behaviour, only to his assumed future plans and ambitions of conquest and aggression. The decision-makers have become the prisoners of their own self-generated worst-case assumptions. It is this 'autistic' siege mentality which also impels them to spare no effort to convince the rest of the nation of the accuracy of their threat perceptions. In these circumstances, an elaborate propaganda machine has been attached to the Military-Industrial Complex, charged with creating an awareness of the values presumed to be under attack and with instilling ordinary citizens with a sense of sacrifice.[11] David M. Shoup, a top-ranking American general until his retirement in 1963, has, in this connection, also drawn attention to the role of veterans' associations in the United States and to the phenomenon of a 'grass-roots militarism'.[12]

However, less work has been done on these 'peripheral' aspects of the MIC than on its various component parts at the centre. Thus, the Federal Budget has been scrutinized to determine the precise share of military expenditure in the U.S. economy.[13] Other analysts have concentrated on the contribution made by arms production to the total turnover of major corporations. It is also well-known that industry and state allocate financial resources to research inside and outside the universities and information has therefore been collected on Research and Development in the military and military-related fields. A good deal of work has also been produced on the role of Congress and the relationship of its members with the Pentagon and with industry. The transnational linkages of the industries involved in arms manufacture have similarly been investigated. This latter line of research led to inquiries into the defense industries of other Western countries, and a number of teams have been engaged in scanning the structure and the operations of MICs in European countries.[14] All these studies taken together would seem to indicate that the Military-Industrial Complex in the broadest sense is not merely an intellectual construct, but a phenomenon that has been empirically verified.

However, none of this empirical work has removed a number of major debating points. First and foremost, there was the problem of the functionality of the MIC. This question had always interested the Marxists, and non-Marxists could not avoid responding to their arguments. But it was also their interest in systems theory which guided influential non-Marxists towards the problem of functionality.[15] If the starting proposition of this theory was correct that systemic entities in general and political systems in particular strive to achieve stability as a condition of their survival over time, then what was the contribution which the existence of a Military-Industrial Complex made to the stabilization of political systems with a high-technology industry? Above all, was it true that capitalism could not do without large-scale armaments, as the Marxists had been arguing since Luxemburg?

It was an argument which other scholars did not find confirmed by their own research. Capitalism, they believed, could survive without high armaments expenditures. Yet this did not imply that the economic weight of the defense sector was insignificant. On the contrary, a good deal of evidence was brought together which showed it to be large enough to make a fundamental reorientation towards civilian production, should it ever be attempted, a precarious and potentially dangerous exercise. There was also little doubt that military expenditure could be used, and was being used, as a device of anti-cyclical economic policy in capitalist countries.[16] Although as a national strategy deficit-spending on armaments was fraught with dangers,[17] it was clear that it had been implemented as an instrument of regional policy in depressed areas in the United States and elsewhere.

The second major area of debate involving Marxists and non-Marxists developed over the question of the presumed stabilising function of the Military-Industrial Complex within the framework of U.S. foreign policy and the effect which American military aid was supposed to have on the political and social structures of allied countries around the world. In the immediate postwar period much of this aid had, of course, been sent to Europe where, together with the Marshall Programme, it was seen to have helped check the threat of revolutionary change. Nor could the reconstruction of Western Europe have succeeded so swiftly, had it not been for the protection which its inclusion in the American sphere of influence afforded it. Work was also done on the impact of U.S. military aid to friendly countries in Latin America, Africa and Asia which provided governments with improved military capabilities not only against external attack, but also against social revolutionary and even reformist forces at home.

Faced with the global scope of U.S. foreign policy, backed as it was by military aid and, occasionally, even direct military intervention, many non-Marxist analysts came to agree with their Marxist colleagues that more than economic advantage was at stake when arms were being exported to developing countries: it was in effect the continued stability of the informal empire which the United States had succeeded in establishing after 1945. The role and influence of the Military-Industrial Complex was therefore seen not merely in the context of the East-West confrontation, but also of the so-called North-South Conflict. American preoccupation with stability, it was agreed, transcended the boundaries of the American political system. On the other hand, few Western scholars were prepared to follow the Norwegian political scientist Johan Galtung without reservations who regarded the managers of the MIC as agents of a global policy of 'structural' violence.[18] In his view, American military and intelligence officers are, overtly or covertly, involved in a permanent campaign against national liberation movements and in quasi-colonial wars. They conduct 'destabilization' operations against 'unfriendly' Third World governments; they arrange arms transfers from the United States and send military advisers and experts to cooperative regimes in Latin America, the Middle East, the Far East and Black Africa, while soldiers from developing countries receive their education and specialized training at Westpoint or Fort Bragg. Galtung has no hesitation in calling these activities militaristic, and, of course, the Marxists would agree with him.

As will be remembered, the pre-1918 Marxist argument had viewed the phenomenon of militarism very much in the context of an 'imperialism as the highest stage of capitalism'.[19] Some 60 years later, one prominent neo-Marxist, the American economist Harry Magdoff of the New School of Social Research, took another look at 'militarism and imperialism' during the annual conference of the American Economic Association in 1970.[20] Magdoff started his paper with a frontal attack upon neo-classical economics in which 'peace reigns supreme' and 'war, militarism and the pacification of natives are treated merely as elements which disturb the harmonious equilibrium models which are to supply us with the universal truths about the allocation of scarce resources'. Marxists, he continued, had by contrast always adhered to the conviction 'that economic processes must be understood as part of a social organism in which political force plays a leading role and in which war is at least as typical as peace'. They would therefore see militarism and imperialism 'as major determinants of the form and direction of technological change, of the allocation of resources within a country and of the allocation of resources between countries (notably between rich and poor countries)'. Consequently, 'price and income relations, treated as ultimate yardsticks of economic efficiency and social justice in neoclassical economics, are viewed, in the Marxist context, as evolutionary products of capitalist institutions in which political force and "pure" economics are intertwined'.

In trying to demonstrate that this latter — Marxist — approach yields a more satisfactory overall interpretation of U.S. involvement in military operations, 'starting from the Revolutionary War and including wars against the Indians, punitive expeditions to Latin America and Asia as well as major wars', he found 'that the United States was engaged in warlike activity during three-fourths of its history, in 1,782 of at least 2,340 months'. To Magdoff it was thus 'no surprise to discover that war-related expenditures have constituted the dominant sector of the federal budget throughout our history'. And, he added, none of this military activity was without a purpose: it 'occurred within a context of empire building, for their has been a continuous thread in U.S. history, beginning with the colonial and revolutionary days, of economic, political and military expansionism directed toward the creation and growth of an American empire.'

Having discussed the various phases within this process of empire-building, Magdoff finally concluded: 'Imperialism necessarily involves militarism. Indeed, they are twins that have fed on each other in the past, as they do now.' Referring to the contemporary period, he was frank enough to admit that 'the greater sophistication of weaponry' had been one reason for the huge increases in military expenditure since the Second World War. However, apart from this factor and, secondly, from that of the military strength of the Soviet Bloc, there was a third element to be included in the evaluation of American policy:

> A substantial portion of the huge military machine, including that of the Western European nations, is the price being paid to maintain the imperialist network of trade and investment in the absence of colonialism. The achievement of political independence by former colonies has stimulated internal class struggles in the new states for economic as well as political independence. Continuing economic dependence of the metropolitan centers within the framework of political independence calls for, among other things, the worldwide dispersion of U.S. military armed forces and the direct military support of the local ruling classes.

To this, he said, must be added 'a) the active promotion of commercial armament sales abroad (contributing a sizeable portion of the merchandise export surplus in recent years); b) the extensive training of foreign military personnel, and c) the use of economic-aid funds to train local police forces for "handling mob demonstrations and counter-intelligence work".'

At the end of his paper Magdoff turned to American domestic politics. In his view, 'this militarism which is working to control the rest of the world is at the same time helping to shape the nature of U.S. society'. He believed much of this impact to be of an economic nature. But it also affected the non-economic relationships between divergent groups inside the United States. Magdoff's concluding statement did not contain a direct political message or an appeal to resort to political action. He merely exhorted his colleagues to recognise the importance of imperialism and militarism as useful tools for analysing the political economy of America. Failure to take account of these factors in economic theory would, he added, 'obscure the truth about the great problems and dangers of the second half of the twentieth century'.

The response to these exhortations has been mixed. The school of 'revisionist' historians who are inspired by the writings of William A. Williams would have no major hesitation in subscribing to key points of the neo-Marxist argument.[21] On the other hand, it was precisely the Williams School and in particular its interpretation of the roots of the Cold War which has been under heavy fire for some time.[22] A similar controversy has arisen in connection with America's involvement in the Vietnam War which some earlier authors had taken to be a typical case of the militarist and imperialist character of U.S. policy. This is not the view of the American historian Guenther Lewy who was able to evaluate large amounts of primary materials for his study on *America in Vietnam*.[23] According to him, Washington's policy in South-East Asia was not part of a coolly calculated strategy, but presented a story of human misperceptions and misjudgements. He found that American decision-makers saw 'the national interest through the fallible spectacles of subjective judgment' and that in assessing 'threats, dangers and interests' they were liable to make mistakes, such as being unduly influenced by '"worst case" calculations or ideological perceptions'.[24] He added: 'The assessment of the geopolitical importance of Vietnam and Southeast Asia by American leaders from 1950 on was an example of such misjudgment'. A strong anti-Communism was one of the factors that warped people's vision. However, according to Lewy there was yet another point: at first, 'with few dissenting voices, American decision-makers considered Vietnam, and indeed all of Southeast Asia, to be of important strategic and economic value to the noncommunist world, but this basic supposition was soon overshadowed by regard for the international and domestic consequences of a loss of Vietnam'. Thenceforth the primary consideration 'became not the importance of a noncommunist South Vietnam in itself, but the repercussions to be expected from reneging on this commitment'. In the international sphere, 'the fear was of disillusionment with the worth of the alliances contracted by the U.S. and the encouragement of other Communist-led "wars of national liberation" which might follow a retreat from Southeast Asia'. As far as the situation at home was concerned, 'the steadfast defense of South Vietnam was to preempt the charge of being soft on communism, an accusation to which Democratic presidents, mindful of Yalta and the "loss of China", were particularly sensitive'.

Not in every case was the counter-argument put forward as subtly and well-supported as in Lewy's book. Nor was it always pertinent and occasionally even amounted to a return to positions which most people thought had long been abandoned in favour of the MIC hypothesis.

Richard Bett's book on the influence of the American military in political decision-making during assorted Cold War crises may be cited as an example here.[25] He considered 'how the proportion of military influence, relative to that of civilian advisers, has varied since World War II'. His findings, he believed, did not

> reinforce either of the common stereotypes of the military role in policy. The left-wing stereotype of military advisers as both fools and knaves — an implicitly inconsistent premise that ascribes to stupid people the power to convince or manipulate smarter ones — falters because military advisers taken as a whole have been less foolish and less powerful than assumed. But neither were they martyrs, shackled and reduced to impotence by appeasing civilian administrators, as the right-wing stereotype suggests. When the soldiers have not been complicit in civilian policy, they have been resourceful in finding ways to resist it. No one who seeks to fix responsibility for disasters in cold war crises by blaming only the military or only the civilians will find comfort in the evidence taken as a whole. There is enough blame to go around for both camps.

Of course, this was never the central issue for those to whom the existence of a Military-Industrial Complex was an incontrovertible fact. They were not interested in separating soldiers from the civilians. On the contrary, they emphasized the collaborative aspect of the civil-military relationship in industrialized countries. Above all, they pointed to the *systemic* character of the problem, and the determinants of American policy-making were seen to lie inside the system.

In the long debate on the role of the American MIC in national and international politics there emerged finally the criticism that both neo-Marxists and 'revisionists' played down the extent to which U.S. policy was influenced by the fact that it was forced to operate within an international milieu of other nation-states with their own foreign policies. Lewy made this point in his book on Vietnam when he asserted that U.S. foreign policy *vis-à-vis* China was 'not the result of an ideological crusade against communism, but was primarily a response to China's attempt to change the status quo. . . by force'.[26] This is the place therefore to examine the behaviour of other superpowers and of the Soviet Union in particular. After all, scholars like Huntington and Senghaas had always assumed that there existed a Military-Industrial Complex in all highly industrialized countries, including Russia.[27] Was Soviet policy governed by impulses very similar to those supposedly guiding the international conduct of the United States? And if so, how did this affect the view of the inner-directedness of American policy-making?

In 1972 the Russian physicist and critic of the Soviet system Andrei Sakharov spoke of a Soviet Military-Industrial Complex which occupied an 'analogous role' to that of the U.S.[28] However, these were merely educated guesses and, as far as can be ascertained, no scholar tried to pursue the theme systematically prior to 1972. It was, of course, well-known that the Soviet Union possessed one of the largest military machines in the world as well as extensive armaments industries, a Research and Development establishment and a firmly entrenched party apparatus. But very little ever filtered through to the West about how these elements functioned within the Soviet system and how they were interrelated. It was also a well-established fact that the Soviet Union was a highly bureaucratized system geared to planning and the implementation of plans. It may have been this general knowledge of the Soviet regime which led the American economist John K. Galbraith to speculate that there existed a 'military-industrial bureaucracy [in Russia] which is concerned with its own perpetuation and growth'.[29] Documentation on this subject has unfortunately always been inadequate, a situation which is quite different from that in the United States. However, attempts have been made to deal with the Soviet case and here reference must be made in the first place to an article which the American social scientist Vernon V. Aspaturian published in 1972 under the title: 'The Soviet Military-Industrial Complex — Does It Exist?'[30]

The most important point in the context of this chapter is that Aspaturian cautiously affirmed earlier generalizations about the existence of an MIC; but he added the proviso that he had defined the concept in its 'broadest sense', i.e. as 'a deliberate and symbiotic sharing of interests on the part of the military establishment, industry and high-ranking political figures whose collective influence is sufficient to shape decisions to accord with the interests of these groups at the expense of others in Soviet society'. In elaborating on this definition, Aspaturian started from the assumption that, Soviet propaganda denials notwithstanding, Russian society was divided into 'interest group formations' which take up divergent positions on particular issues.

Among the most important of these issues, he continued, were 'those concerned with the allocation of resources'. This led to various interests 'to crystallize into distinctive demand sectors of which there are principally six' in the Soviet Union: '1) the *ideological demand* sector (the ideologues and conservatives of the Party apparatus); 2) the *security demand* sector (the police, armed forces and defense industries)'; the latter, he continued, overlaps to some extent with 3)

the *producer demand* sector (heavy industry, construction and trans-
portation)'; there is '4) the *consumer demand* sector (light industry,
consumer goods industry, trade and housing); 5) the *agricultural demand*
sector; and 6) the *public services and welfare* sector.' Aspaturian then
argued that 'Soviet policy, domestic and foreign, responds primarily to
internal constituencies, although residual response to external constituencies (foreign communist parties, communist states and the international communist movement) continues to persist in some degree'.
This 'steady orientation of Soviet policy toward internal constituencies' had produced 'a polarization of men and institutions into a
security-producer-ideological grouping and a consumer-agricultural-
public services grouping'.

In view of this bipolarity, it is not difficult to see the contours
of a Soviet Military-Industrial Complex emerging from Aspaturian's
analysis. It consisted of '1) the armed forces; 2) the defense industries
complex and related research and development institutions; 3) heavy
industry; and 4) the conservative wing of the Party apparatus'. Much of
the rest of the author's analysis was then concerned with the patterns of
interaction between (1) and (2) above which he identified as the two
'core' factors of the Soviet Military-Industrial Complex and finally led
him to propose that

> what ties the major components of the Soviet military-industrial
> complex together is their understanding of the interdependency
> that exists between security, heavy industry and ideological ortho-
> doxy. This perception of interdependence is a complex political
> relationship, one that transcends the simplistic formula that
> security requires the primacy of heavy industry and ideological
> controls, since heavy industrial interests would continue to favor
> the primacy of heavy industry and conservative Party people
> would continue to favor tight ideological controls regardless of
> security considerations.

At the end of his article Aspaturian raised the question of what kept
the MIC in its powerful position. In principle, he felt, 'the need for
preserving the existing structure of priorities can find its stimulus
internally as well as externally', even if the 'justification for the continued primacy of defense and heavy industry can only originate
externally'. But on the assumption that the need was stimulated internally, it would be clear that 'the military and industrial bureaucracies
are less institutions serving defense and foreign policy interests than
entities being served by a particular defense and foreign policy posture'.
Hence Aspaturian's conclusion: 'If this be true, the Soviet military and
heavy industry constitute a military-industrial complex not only in the

physical sense but, in conjunction with the conservative Party leaders, constitute one in the political sense as well.'

These statements rattled the Frankfurt political scientist Egbert Jahn sufficiently to question the legitimacy of analysing all MICs within one and the same framework, irrespective of a country's socio-economic structure. He wanted the systemic differences between America and Russia to be taken more seriously than Aspaturian had done.[31] He was convinced that the absence, in the Soviet Union, of a 'private-capitalist interest in profit-making' with its resultant search for new markets, especially overseas, created tangible divergencies from the American model. However, in 1973 he was not yet, as he admitted, in a position to offer a satisfactory answer to what were 'the socio-economic interests behind the global strategic expansion of the Soviet Union'. Subsequently a team of researchers headed by Jahn at the Frankfurt Institute for Peace and Conflict Research brought together more material which they published in the late 1970s.[32] This work represented the first attempt to come to terms, in a more carefully conducted analysis, with the problems posed by Aspaturian.

Jahn's most significant conclusion was that it was dangerous simply to transpose to the Soviet Union a concept, which had been devised to deal with certain phenomena in American society. He proposed to use the term 'Military-Bureaucratic Complex' (MBC) instead. Only this concept, he believed, was capable of taking account of the fact that Russia is a society in which the means of production are owned by the state, which is thoroughly bureaucratized in a hierarchical fashion and dominated by a powerful Party apparatus. Moreover, whereas the American system is characterized by publicly competing organized and informal interest groups, Party control is all-pervasive in the Soviet Union. There are no political groups which openly challenge and criticise the CPSU's official military policy and the economic priorities laid down by it, as Jahn's evaluation of the Soviet military press demonstrated. Although it was clearly differentiated from the civilian press in terms of organization and personnel, Party control of the military press was almost total. Important articles were written not by professional military people, but by *komissars* who were part of the Party apparatus. At most, the military press therefore reflects military interests indirectly, in so far as the Party felt disposed to respond to military preoccupations and to give them an airing.

On the other hand, Jahn did not go so far as to regard the Soviet bureaucratic system as monolithic and dominated by one single factor; nor as totally immobile. However, any shifts that were discernible were provided not by conflicts between different organized interest groups, as in the United States, but resulted exclusively from intra-bureaucratic rivalries and from tensions between the state bureaucracy and the unorganized mass of the population. Since the latter was largely unable to articulate its views, any criticism of policy positions has to come from inside an organization, i.e. the bureaucracy itself whose rigid hierarchical structure erects considerable barriers against the formulation of policy alternatives. All this, Jahn concluded, added up to the marked conservatism of the Soviet MBC. This conservatism had become reinforced by the historical experience of a genuine external threat posed by the greater dynamism of capitalist-industrial societies. Jahn would attach considerable weight to the collective memories of the Russians and their leaders of outside intervention which more than once since 1917 threatened the regime with extinction. This experience, he maintained, largely explains the influence of military considerations in Soviet policy-making and the persistence of a fortress mentality among Russian bureaucrats.

An attempt to move away from the notion of a monolithic Soviet regime and to penetrate the facade of the civil-military relationship has also been made recently by Roman Kolkowicz of UCLA and by the Canadian political scientist Timothy Colton.[33] Kolkowicz has been interested for some time in what he views as the phenomenon of permanent conflict between the CPSU and the armed forces.[34] To him the Soviet marshals are a pressure group constantly struggling to gain greater managerial autonomy and hence confronting the Party with the need to control it. Colton, on the other hand, doubts that there exists a serious control problem of this kind and advances a 'participation model'. In his view, the Party is quite prepared to let the armed forces manage their internal affairs and to allow them to participate in decision-making. Conflict is avoided because the Party generally sets goals which the marshals can subscribe to. Consequently they are deemed to possess a good deal of autonomy, but — thanks to Party policy — do not feel the need to intervene particularly vigorously. They are quite satisfied to be involved to the extent they are.

But as has happened so often in this debate, both approaches have been criticized, in particular by William E. Odom, a former White House expert on East European affairs. He believes that the salient feature of the Soviet civil-military relationship is not conflict, but 'a congruence in organizational ethos'.[35] As to the absence of sharp conflict between the Party and the armed forces which Colton examined in his study, Odom advances a different explanation. He sees it

> rooted in the historical development of the Russian imperial
> state and the heritage of the multinational empire it bequeathed

the Bolsheviks. . . Lenin faced up to the politics of ruling a state that embraces very powerful centrifugal forces. As long as those forces persist, the military imperatives for Soviet rule shall remain dominant for the CPSU. The CPSU is not beholden unto corporate military interest; rather it understands military-bureaucratic requisites for ruling the Soviet Union. It is not paying off the military corporate interests to get the marshals to behave; rather it is emphasizing military power to cope with political realities. The marshals cannot afford the luxury of corporate military interests; they are in the same boat with the CPSU.[36]

Although Odom does not use Jahn's MBC terminology, key elements of their conceptual framework are nevertheless quite similar. Nor would both authors hesitate to call Russia 'militaristic'. However, it is doubtful if they would find themselves in agreement over the applicability of the concept to the *American* system. For, whatever the twists and turns in the MIC debate, ultimately it involved fundamental political positions to which we must now come back at the end of this chapter.

The Marxist position on this issue is the most straightforward one and need not be recapitulated here. The non-Marxists present a more varied picture. What the most modest critics of the Military-Industrial Complex have in effect been concerned with was the wasting of valuable resources and the militarization of American foreign policy by a small elite. Their analysis implied that it was possible to reallocate these resources to satisfy civilian needs and to demilitarize diplomacy without turning the country's existing socio-economic structures upside-down. In many ways, this position is reminiscent of that of the Radicals in the pre-1914 Liberal Party in Britain and of J.A. Hobson's critique of nineteenth-century British imperialism: the problem was not industrial capitalism *per se*, but certain maladjustments.[37] In the present-day context, it is the notion of a high-technology military-industrial factor whose emergence since the Second World War is seen to have resulted in fresh distortions of the system and in false priorities. They could be, and indeed had to be, corrected if capitalism was to be saved from collapse.

This liberal-reformist position assumed that there existed counter-forces in Western society which could be mobilized against the military-industrial elite before it became a serious danger to the stability of society as a whole. Quite consistently the critique of the Military-Industrial Complex was therefore frequently coupled with a demand to curb its power. Nor is it a coincidence that this position, which had a long tradition in the Anglo-Saxon world, gained considerable

popularity in the wake of the Vietnam War and the general crisis of
conscience of the late 1960s and early 1970s. Even the writings of a
seemingly more radical author like Senghaas ought to be seen in the
broader political context of a belief that there existed, in this period of
moral bankruptcy of the highly technological 'civilian militarism'[38], a
genuine chance to initiate a policy which aimed at the reduction of the
burden of armaments and the use of scarce resources for improvements
of the social infrastructure. As Galbraith put it, military influences
on policy-making were to cut down to their traditional size.[39] The
financial savings were to be used for social reform.

There was a further position which in some respects pre-dated the
debate on the MIC and which was powerfully represented by C.W.
Mills. He tended to be more sceptical of the presumed anti-militaristic
potential of modern industrial societies and regarded the *Power Elite*
as homogeneous and firmly entrenched. He was also convinced that
the influence of the military was rising and that its policies would result
in a further escalation of the arms race and, ultimately, in World War
III:[40]

> Everywhere now there are the generals and the captains who, by
> their presence, create and maintain a militarist atmosphere.
> Professional economists usually consider military institutions as
> parasitic upon the means of economic production. Now, however,
> military institutions and aims have come to shape much of the
> economic life of the United States, without which the war machine
> could not exist. Religion, virtually without exception blesses the
> nation at war, and recruits from among its officials the chaplain,
> who in military costume eases the conscience and stiffens the
> morale of men at war. Military men have entered political and
> diplomatic circles; they have gone into the higher echelons of the
> corporate economy; they have taken charge of scientific and
> technological endeavor; they have influenced higher educational
> institutions; they are operating a truly enormous public-relations
> and propaganda machinery. The rise of the warlords to enlarged
> command and increased status is but the most obvious sign of the
> fact that decisions of the greatest consequence have become
> largely international, and that the economics and the politics of
> international affairs are regularly defined in terms of the military
> metaphysic. For the professional military, domestic policies are
> important mainly as ways of retaining and enlarging the military
> establishment.

Mills had no doubt that 'militarism' was the appropriate term to
describe these processes which he believed to be at work in modern
industrial society. On this score, other writers were prepared to agree

with him, even if they did not share his pessimism. Senghaas entitled his volume *Armaments and Militarism*.[41] Although his empirical material is primarily American, he clearly also had the Soviet Union in mind. In his view, militarism existed tendentially in all modern high-technology countries, capitalist or socialist. Lasswell, in his 1962 reappraisal of his 'Garrison State Hypothesis'[42], was more inclined to consider the Soviet regime militaristic, with the United States being on the way towards it. Other authors have continued to display a certain reluctance to use the concept at all. Instead they speak of *Weapons Culture*[43], *Warfare State*[44] or *Pentagon Capitalism*[45] when analysing high-technology societies.

Does this mean that the debate on militarism is no nearer to a generally accepted definition in 1979 than it was a hundred years ago? This must certainly be the conclusion in the strict sense, and it is for this reason that no attempt will be made to come up with a fresh definition here. However, the debate since Proudhon, as summarized in this volume, does suggest agreement on a typology of militarism which will be presented and tested in the following chapter.

Notes

1   See his article, with H. Mommsen, in the encyclopedia *Sowjetsystem und demokratische Gesellschaft*, Vol. 4, Freiburg-Basel-Wien 1971, Col. 561.

2   In *U.S. Department of State Bulletin*, No. 1128, 1961, pp.179-82.

3   See the bibliography below, pp. 125ff.

4   D. Senghaas, *Rüstung und Militarismus*, Frankfurt 1972, p.14.

5   V.K. Dibble, 'The Garrison Society.' *New University Thought* 5 (1966/67), Special Issue.

6   C.W. Mills, *The Power Elite*, New York 1956.

7   M. Pilisuk and T. Hayden, 'Is There a Military-Industrial Complex Which Prevents Peace?' *Journal of Social Issues*, 21 (July 1965), p.67.

8   D. Senghaas, *Rüstung und Militarismus*, p.14.

9   Ibid., p 16

10   Ibid., pp.50ff. The problem of perceptions of reality has also been pursued by authors like R.J. Barnet and G. Lewy. See below pp. 93f.

11   See, e.g., J.W. Fulbright, *The Pentagon Propaganda Machine*, New York 1970

12   D.M. Shoup, 'The New American Militarism.' *The Atlantic Monthly* 223 (April 1969), pp.51-56.

13   A useful summary of this work and the research described below is contained in S. Rosen, ed., *Testing the Theory of the Military-Industrial Complex*, Teakfield 1973. See also C.W. Pursell jr., ed., *The Military-Industrial Complex*, New York 1972.

14   See in particular the work done by the *Hessische Stiftung Friedens- und Konfliktforschung* at Frankfurt.

15   For early, more detailed formulations of this theory see the studies by K. Deutsch and D. Easton, to mention but two important authors.

16   Hjalmar Schacht's experiments in this field of Nazi economic policy after 1933

are of particular interest here. For details see, e.g., the section by W. Sauer in K.D. Bracher et al., *Die national-sozialistische Machtergreifung*, Cologne 1962, pp. 785ff.

17   The problems which the Nazi economy ran into are the best example of these dangers. See below pp. 114f.

18   See D. Senghaas, ed., *Kritische Friedensforschung*, Frankfurt 1971, p.57.

19   See above pp. 25f.

20   H. Magdoff, *'Militarism and Imperialism'. American Economic Review* 60 (May 1970), Papers and Proceedings, pp. 237-42.

21   W.A. Williams, *The Tragedy of American Diplomacy*, New York 1959. See also G. Kolko, *The Politics of War*, New York 1968; L.C. Gardner, *Architects of Illusion*, Chicago 1970; G. Alperovitz, *Atomic Strategy*, New York 1965.

22   See, e.g., R.J. Maddox, *The New Left and the Origins of the Cold War*, Princeton 1973; G.C. Herring, *Aid to Russia, 1941-1946*, New York 1973; R.S. Kirkendall, ed., *The Human Period as a Research Field*, Columbia (Missouri) 1974, G. Kurland, ed., *The Failure of Diplomacy*, New York 1975.

23   G. Lewy, *America in Vietnam*, New York 1978. For another recent reassessment by a large variety of authors see A. Lake, ed., *The Vietnam Legacy*, New York 1976.

24   G. Lewy, *America*, p. 422. This is also a major theme of Richard J. Barnet's writings. See, esp., his *Roots of War*, Baltimore 1973. Very good also: D. Yergin, *Shattered Peace*, Boston 1977.

25   R.K. Betts, *Soldiers, Statesmen and Cold War Crises*, Cambridge (Mass.) 1977, pp.1-2. Broader in scope, but also trying to take a 'middling' position is, e.g., J.L. Gaddis, *The United States and the Origins of the Cold War*, New York 1972.

26   G. Lewy, *America*, p.420.

27   See S.P. Huntington's contribution to the *International Encyclopedia of the Social Sciences*, Vol. 2, New York 1968, p.494; D. Senghaas, 'Rüstungsdynamik in Ost und West.' *Gewaltfreie Aktion* 4 (1972), p.80.

28   A. Sakharov, *Postscript to 1972 Memorandum*, June 1972, reprinted in *Die Zeit*, 21.7.1972, p.4.

29   J.K. Galbraith, *How to Control the Military*, New York (1969), p.22.

30   V.V. Aspaturian, 'The Soviet Military-Industrial Complex — Does It Exist?' *Journal of International Affairs* 26 (1972), pp. 1-28.

31   E. Jahn et al., *Problems of the Analysis of Soviet Security Policy*, mimeogr. MS, Frankfurt 1973.

32   E. Jahn, *Rüstung und Bürokratie in der Sowjetgesellschaft*, mimeogr. MS, Frankfurt 1977.

33   R. Kolkowicz, 'Interest Groups in Soviet Politics: The Case of the Military,' in: D.R. Herspring and I. Volgyes eds., *Civil-Military Relations in Communist Systems*, Boulder 1978, pp.9-25; T.J. Colton, 'The Party-Military Connection: A Participatory Model', in: ibid., pp. 53-75. See also T.J. Colton, *Commissars, Commanders and Civilian Authority*, Cambridge (Mass.) 1979.

34   A more extensive version of his essay first appeared in 1970. See also his book *The Soviet Military and the Communist Party*, Princeton 1967. For additional information on the role of the Red Army in Soviet politics see E.L. Warner III, *The Military in Contemporary Soviet Politics*, New York 1977. Warner's is an 'institutional analysis' based on a bureaucratic politics approach and hence more generally relevant to the MBC debate. He even succeeds in showing that the armed forces themselves do not represent a united bloc. Overall he appears

to agree with the Kolkowicz hypothesis.

35 W.E. Odom, 'The Party-Military Connection: A Critique' in: D.R. Herspring and I. Volgyes, eds., *Civil-Military Relations*, pp.27-52.
36 Ibid., p.48.
37 See above pp. 18f.
38 D. Senghaas, *Rüstung und Militarismus*, p. 23.
39 J.K. Galbraith, *How to Control the Military*.
40 C.W. Mills, *The Causes of World War Three*, London 1959, pp.59f.
41 D. Senghaas, *Rüstung und Militarismus*.
42 See above pp. 45ff.
43 R.E. Lapp, *The Weapons Culture*, New York 1968.
44 F. Cook, *The Warfare State*, New York 1962.
45 S. Melman, *Pentagon Capitalism*, New York 1970.

VI   Towards a Definition:
The Two Types of Militarism

If one abandons the broadly chronologial approach which we have taken so far and tries to systematize the various currents of thought on the subject of militarism, Gerhard Ritter's writings, which have been analyzed in Chapter III, present a suitable starting point.[1]* What typefied the mode of analysis which he revived after the Second World War was its narrow focus, the restriction not merely to Germany, but to politics and diplomacy. As we have seen, he and those historians who wrote in the same vein saw the problem of militarism primarily in terms of the position of the army *vis-à-vis* the state; and the state, in turn, was conceived as an abstract entity, divorced from society, very much in the German philosophical tradition.[2] He was preoccupied with the question of how far the armed forces became a state within the state in Prussia-Germany and how they were able, from this position of exclusiveness, to wield a decisive influence on the country's external behaviour. For, again following a German tradition dating back to Leopold von Ranke, Ritter viewed the state first and foremost as an actor operating within the existing international system and jockeying to secure its survival in the Machiavellian world of power politics. Militarism emerged whenever the military aspect of politics became a state's overriding concern and wherever the (real or alleged) technical necessities of the preparation for war gained the upper hand over considerations of 'the steady art of statecraft'.[3] It is at this point that the civil-military relationship became 'unhealthy'.

   In so far as any other factor was taken into account by Ritter, it was 'democracy'. The 'masses', acting in combination with the militarists of the self-enclosed Army, were, in his view, responsible for throwing overboard the idea of *raison d'état* as a guiding principle of Germany's foreign policy and for pushing the entire country into an orgy of militarism. It is not too difficult to see that this approach to the problem would wind up with a fairly narrow definition of the phenomenon. The emphasis on *raison d'état* and international politics cut out from the analysis the entire domestic arena of politics, whereas the term 'the masses' was useless as a sociological category. Its lack of precision certainly contributed to blocking the path along which Ritter might have ventured into other areas of historical reality.

Yet, it would be improper and unfair to consign Ritter's work on the subject to the dustheap of historical writing. To begin with, whatever the limitations of his approach, he did point up one aspect of our problem which the American modernization theorists of the 1950s were prone to overlook when analyzing the position of the military in Third World countries: it was the fact that nation states and societies do not operate in a vacuum, but act in an international milieu. It was consistent with Ritter's approach that he should give primary importance to the external pressures of geography and military as well as political power exerted by other countries. But at least he was not oblivious of the problem that other nations do interfere with the internal development of an individual state and may, to some extent, even influence the adoption, by that state, of a militaristic policy.

The other point to be remembered about his interpretation is that it was not all that far removed from a strand of Anglo-Saxon thought on the subject of militarism to which repeated reference has been made in earlier chapters. Certainly the older Western discussion on civil-military relations had also remained primarily in the realm of politics and had focused on what constituted the proper balance between the political sphere and the position of the military in a given country. The difference was, however, that the political sphere was not seen as something abstract in a German tradition. Unlike German theory, Anglo-Saxon political thought on the whole did not conceive of the state as an entity above, and divorced from, society. To raise the question of the civil-military relationship was therefore always and at the same time to inquire into the position of the armed forces *vis-à-vis* and within civilian society. To quote Huntington again:[4] 'The principal focus of civil-military relations is the relation of the officer corps and the state'. But, he added immediately, 'the social and economic relations between the military and the rest of society normally reflect the political relations between the officer corps and the state'.

It was along this avenue that Huntington and other writers were now able to advance towards an analysis of socio-economic structures in which, implicitly at least, Western social scientists had been interested since Spencer. Like Marx and his followers, Spencer postulated an antinomy between a 'militant type of society' and an industrial one. These two societies were characterized by different principles of political and economic organization and a correspondingly different value system.[5] As we have seen, Spencer's scheme was quite simple and , if stripped down to its bare essentials, in effect concerned with the political economies of feudal-agrarian societies, on the one hand, and of liberal-capitalist industrialism, on the other. Historical 'Progress' would then see to it that the former was eventually replaced by the latter, and with it militarism would also disappear. The Marxists, it will remembered, similarly expected the dialectical march of History to take care of the problem of militarism, but only one stage beyond the Spencerian evolution of society, i.e. under communism. The capitalist-industrial phase of History, on the other hand, was just as militaristic as earlier historical periods had been.

In 1917, then, a regime emerged in Russia which claimed to have taken the decisive leap from capitalism to socialism. Yet, the 'building of communism', which has been going on in the Soviet Union for more than 60 years now, has not made it any easier for us to come to grips with the phenomenon of militarism. On the positive side, there has been a rapprochement between Marxists and non-Marxists to the extent that Ritter's theory finds but few advocates these days. Whatever their ideological predilections, today the overwhelming majority of scholars tries to relate the whole complex of the civil-military relationship to the socio-economic structures of the country in question. The Western debate both on the role of armies in developing countries and on the Military-Industrial Complex provide ample evidence of this focal interest. The Marxists have never denied its importance. On the other hand, a fresh disagreement has been added to the discussion between divergent schools of thought: that over the nature of the Soviet 'Military-Industrial Complex'. And on this front, as we have seen[6], the battle-lines are not clearly drawn between Marxists and non-Marxists.

Nevertheless, all participants in the debate would probably agree that our understanding of the problem has not only become more sophisticated, but has also undergone a marked shift of emphasis. In trying to take account of this, Senghaas has put forward the argument that an *extended* notion of militarism is required for an analysis of contemporary trends. But it has already been suggested above that we are really talking about two *different* types of militarism. This is the moment to elaborate on this difference.

If one looks at the writings on the subject of militarism which have been reviewed in the first *four* chapters of this volume, it becomes clear that they were all taking their material from countries that were making their transition from an agrarian to an industrial society. Furthermore, this transition took place within the framework of political institutions which were autocratic and oligarchical. In those cases where representative government and a modern system of interest representation existed, they had not yet firmly established themselves. Germany and Japan in the late nineteenth and early twentieth centuries offer particularly striking examples of countries experiencing rapid social and economic change which their preindustrial political systems and power-structures found difficult to absorb and accommodate. While this incongruity between economic and political development created instability and tension at home, another marked feature of both countries was that they developed expansionist aspirations aiming at the establishment of formal empires by means of external aggression. There can be little doubt that a connection existed between the state of latent or even open civil war within these transitional societies and those aggressive designs.

However, the crucial point is that all the above-mentioned older interpretations of militarism had in effect the cases of these transitional societies in front of them. Woodrow Wilson echoed the theories built upon these examples in 1916 when lecturing at West Point. 'Militarism', he said, 'does not consist of any army, nor even of the existence of a very great army. Militarism is a spirit. It is a point of view. It is a purpose. The purpose of militarism is to use armies for aggression'.[7] In his 1972 analysis of the 'present-day problem of militarism' in high-technology countries, Senghaas, as might be expected, arrived at a similar conclusion. He cited William James as one of his witnesses who had asserted in 1910 that war and the 'competitive preparation' for it were synonyms[8]. These developments, Senghaas added, had been anticipated before 1945, but 'achieved a breakthrough under politically and technologically modified conditions only after 1945'. Yet, have these and other conditions not changed beyond recognition?

To begin with, the weapons technologies of the highly industrialized countries have become so destructive that major wars between those nations no longer present a genuine policy option. The use of nuclear weapons in a push-button confrontation would end in the destruction not only of the opponent, but also of the attacker. At the same time there has been a notable change in political conditions. If Wilson was correct in assuming that the 'spiritual' element is an essential ingredient of militarism, it appears to be absent from the 'mass politics' of the high-technology countries whose populations adhere overwhelmingly to a civilian life-style. They are consumer-orientated and openly fearful of war. There is no popular enthusiasm for paramilitarism and for programmes of territorial expansion. Attempts to organize people in militaristic associations meet, in so far as they are undertaken at all, with little success. War is not heroicized and elevated in a Jünger-style literature.

This does not mean to imply that the term is no longer applicable to developed industrial societies. Militarism has assumed a new quality owing to the decline of features that were, and are, typical of the militarism of *industrializing* societies and, conversely, owing to the appearance of features which developing societies did not, and do not, possess. This conclusion is partly drawn from what has been said in earlier chapters. However, it seems possible to test it further. Was there perhaps a time in history when the two types of militarism began to overlap and were found to be incompatible in the process? If this can be shown, it would point to precisely the qualitative difference that is being postulated here.

Before looking at our test case it seems useful to recall Harold Lasswell's 'Garrison State Hypothesis'.[9] As has been seen, his scheme in effect amounted to an amalgam of the older type of militarism (characterized by a 'spiritual' mass militarism, military-dominated political processes and warmongering) and a Senghaasian high-technology industrial militarism. The country which Lasswell evidently had in mind as the place where this ominous mixture was being prepared was Nazi Germany. He contrasted this emerging 'Garrison State' with a western-style 'Business State' which, though possessing a modern technology, lacked militaristic mass mobilization as well as domination by the 'specialists on violence'. Writing in 1940/41, at the height of Hitler's success, Lasswell may be forgiven for believing that the blending of a high-technology militarism with that of developing societies would offer a lasting solution, albeit a spine-chilling one. We now know enough not only about the downfall of the Nazi system four years later, but also about its structural weaknesses and inbuilt contradictions that we are in a position to say that it did not work.

However, before we present this story of failure and self-destruction, it is necessary to demonstrate that a militarism of the kind analyzed in the chapter on the 'Military-Industrial Complex' had begun to exist in Germany side-by-side with what might be called the militarism of 'traditional' and transitional societies. By way of reference to the phenomenon of paramilitarism and to the militaristic literature of the interwar period a good deal has already been said about the latter, with the study by James Diehl providing a fuller summary of *Paramilitary Politics in Weimar Germany*.[10] His book deals with the millions of Germans who joined Weimar's militaristic private armies. The recent work of Michael Geyer, on the other hand, goes into the former brand of militarism.[11] Significantly enough, it was conceived in the Reichswehr Ministry at Berlin. The traditional view of the Reichswehr has been that it developed into a 'state within the state' and that, by fostering paramilitary associations and a revanchist propaganda, while at the same time throwing its political weight about, it resumed the role of the pre-1914 Prussian Army.[12] General Hans von Seeckt, the father of the Weimar Army, held impeccably conservative views about its organization and function in society. His approach was elitist-exclusivist, hostile to the existing parliamentary regime and with little appreciation of the lessons to be learned from the First World War in the fields of technology and economics. In short, he stood for the ideas and principles of the old Prussian Army.

What was true of Seeckt, was not necessarily true of the majors and colonels on his staff. According to Geyer, much of what has been written about the Reichswehr since 1945 represents merely half the picture. His evaluation of fresh archival material revealed a different and very 'modern' image of the German army. He discovered that there had been a number of younger officers in the planning and operations departments of the Ministry who had drawn their own conclusions from the course of the First World War. Whereas many of their older comrades were convinced that the war had been lost by Germany because of a breakdown in her morale and 'will power', the 'industrialization of warfare' left an indelible impression on the planners in the young Republic's military bureaucracy. These officers saw themselves as professionals devoted to putting an end to the chaos and decentralization which marked the organization of the Reichswehr in the early 1920s.

So they began to improve the system of mobilization and to rationalize logistics in an attempt to gear Germany's armed forces to the age of high mechanization and automation of warfare. The following example may be seen to put the concern with questions of modern technology and of the most economic deployment of resources into a nutshell. It arose from the fact that the First World War had demonstrated the potential of an air force and that protection against air attack was likely to be vital in the future. Accordingly, the Reichswehr Ministry drew up plans for a nationwide air raid warning service. But one of the local commanders thought it important to give the members of this service a traditional military training in addition to the specialized instruction provided. The Ministry sent him a severe reprimand saying that the air raid protection personnel should learn 'to use the telephone rather than to fight'.[13] It was in this way that the young professionals tried to overcome the traditionalism, improvisation and lack of direction at all levels which had characterized the early postwar period. While drafting their statistical tables and organization charts, they quickly came to realise that, if their activities were to be successful, they could not do without the cooperation and support of the civilian authorities. The old notion of the Army existing as a state within the state had to be abandoned. The Army had to become an integral part of the Republic.

This change of attitude and policy resulted in new links with industry and the civilian authorities. It also resulted in discreet lobbying of deputies and other politicians; in matter-of-fact presentation of military problems to committees rather than shrill propaganda. In short, the Ministry developed a style of military politics and interest representation the essential features of which were quite similar to the practices of modern military establishments today. Even if civil-military tensions did not disappear altogether, they certainly lost much of their former bitterness and the Reichswehr now participated in public sector planning as a matter of course. It proved to be an effective lobbyist, and there were also growing connections with industry.[14] When Helmuth von Moltke, the Chief of the General Staff, was asked in 1914 what kind of economic preparations had been made for the war that had just started, he refused to be bothered with such trivia. 'We have to fight a war now', was his bland reply. The staff officers in the Reichswehr Ministry took a very different view and were acutely aware of the need for a well-oiled economy as a prerequisite of successful military planning, and not just in wartime. Consequently, cooperation extended not only to the civilian bureaucracy, but also to industry.

This brief summary of Geyer's findings may suffice to indicate that there was a sharp contrast between these activities and the noisy anti-Republican agitation and tiresome copying of Prussian Army drill on the part of Germany's paramilitary leagues. The planners and lobbyists in Berlin were engaged in seemingly normal operations which were 'never openly politicized and received no airing in public'. In view of this, Geyer wonders whether historians have been concentrating for too long on the militarism of the Republic's *Wehrverbände* and intellectuals, while ignoring the work of the 'skilled professional organizers and strategists' in Berlin. The crucial point is that by the early 1930s the two had begun to coexist very uneasily. The military technocrats were eyed with distrust by the associations. The former, in turn, found their aims and policies to be at variance with those of the private armies and manoeuvred to contain them.

Compromise was reached in January 1933 when Hitler came to power. His aim was the total mobilization of society with all its human and material resources. Accordingly, the years after 1933 were the heyday of the military planners who prepared the expansion of the Wehrmacht from the 100,000-men force of Weimar to the large army of 1939.[15] In close collusion with the civilian bureaucracy and German industry, they also built up a large military-industrial empire in which the technological foundations were laid for the mechanized campaigns of Hitler's wars of aggression in 1939/41. All in all, the whole rearmament programme went as well as could be expected given the size of the task. Some historians, it is true, have been struck by the anarchy and confusion which appeared to be reigning in the Third Reich.[16] No doubt the regime was vexed by innumerable interdepartmental rows over competences and priorities. Yet, although this aspect of Nazi reality has been a major focus of discussion in recent years, it looks as if the degree of collaboration which was actually achieved between various agencies has been underrated. The dynamics of Hitler's system of government cannot be understood without the devotion and enthusiasm with which the professionals in the armed forces went about their work together with the managers of industry, party functionaries, architects and other highly-trained specialists to secure the smooth execution of a technological and technocratic militarism.

If the planners and managers encountered one serious problem in their concerted effort to arm the country, it was not bureaucratic rivalry and chaos, but lack of funds adequate to the objective of territorial expansion. In 1939/40 Hitler astonished and frightened the world with his successful lightning campaigns against Germany's eastern and western neighbours. Only after 1945 did it become clearer that the wars against Poland and in the West were much less the products of brilliant strategic thinking than of dire necessity. Economically and militarily, the country was merely ready for short thrusts forward.[17] No expensive rearmament 'in depth' had taken place.

Meanwhile a plausible explanation for this omission has been found: in-depth rearmament would have required the introduction of an austerity programme which Hitler and his advisers did not dare to adopt;[18] for it was not that they would not have preferred austerity to their actual policy. On the contrary, the idea of sacrifice and discipline in the interest of 'the survival of the nation' was part and parcel of the theory of total mobilization for war to which the Nazis subscribed. As General Erich Ludendorff put it in his book on *Total War*, published in 1935, survival in the struggle between empires and races was 'a matter not only for the armed forces, but touched upon the life and soul of every single member of the warring nations'.[19] Ideally, therefore, the population was to be prepared in peacetime for actively supporting a future war. Indoctrination with militaristic values was to put them in a mood of sacrifice and cheerful acceptance of military service. The Nazi theory of the psychological preparation for war revealed behind its emotional language a notion of militarism which we have associated with transitional societies. It was a militarism which claimed absolute primacy of military considerations over politics and aimed at pervading society with a warlike spirit. The journalist Josef Winschuh provided a particularly neat summary of the Nazi ideal when he wrote in 1939/40:[20]

> National Socialism guarantees that this unity [of soldiers and workers] will be continued and deepened. Under its guidance, the attitude of the worker can and will no longer constitute a threat to the spirit of the soldier. Rather a valuable cross-fertilization is taking place. Through its technical weapons, the Army is incorporating into itself the know-how and proud efficiency (*sachlichen Leistungsstolz*) of the skilled worker. But it absorbs these qualities into its soldierly spirit. On the other hand, it is part of National Socialist education to instil the worker increasingly with a soldierly spirit. A special relationship exists between the soldier and the armaments worker. We are so fortunate as to possess an armaments industry whose quality and reputation is as high as that of our Army. . . .War is conducted by soldiers who do the fighting and by "soldiers of labour" who create the arms.

Had this synthesis ever been seriously attempted, the regime, if successful, would have been able to rely on mass support for an austerity programme, and full-scale rearmament 'in depth' might have been economically possible. However, the attempt to attune the population to the values of a martial society geared to policies of territorial conquest remained half-hearted. One reason for this hesitation was related to Hitler's foreign policy in the early years after 1933.[21] Preoccupied with consolidating his domestic position and with establishing a dictatorial hold over a society in which the traditonal elites still wielded considerable power and the working class had been well-organized, he could not afford to get entangled in diplomatic confrontations with other powers. One way of undercutting hostile foreign reaction was for him to pose as a statesman of moderation and an apostle of peace. This strategy worked well enough to calm anxieties which existed abroad about his *Lebensraum* ambitions, but suffered from the drawback that it also influenced domestic opinion in a pacifist direction. A policy of spiritual mobilization for total war could not be carried out full steam while Hitler was launching his peace initiatives.

There was another and possibly more important reason for his restraint: the attempt to create a total war society would not just have threatened Nazi foreign policy, but the stability of the regime as a whole. There are two reasons for this. The first relates to the position of Ernst Röhm's SA, the Brownshirts. In many ways this paramilitary arm of the Nazi Party embodied the 'political soldierdom' of the Movement, absolutely devoted to its violent aims both at home and abroad. Röhm and his followers saw themselves not merely as street-fighters who restored 'law and order' in the country, but also as the hardcore of politicized mass army.[22] The SA had grown out of the Free Corps of the post-revolutionary period and, partly because of this tradition, had developed a revolutionary image of itself.[23] When, after Hitler's seizure of power, it became a mass organization comprising three million members, Röhm's *mélange* of militarism and radical politics became highly explosive. He claimed that the Brownshirts represented the 'true ideals' of National Socialism and that the political leadership in Germany belonged to them.

Consequently, by 1934, the SA posed a serious political threat not only to the Army as the sole guardian of military professionalism and rearmament, but also to Hitler. The murder of Röhm and his en-tourage in the Night of the Long Knives on 30 June 1934 effectively eliminated the Brownshirts as a threat to the regime.[24] Nevertheless, their rise and activities in the early 1930s exposed the dangers inherent in a democratized paramilitarism. It was difficult to control and was liable to exert a destabilizing influence upon a regime which, for the sake of its own cohesion, was heavily dependent on the *Führer* principle. The history of the SA shows that the 'Garrison State' was constantly being threatened 'from below' by the radical forces of organized militarism it had been nourishing.

However, there emerged, also at grass-roots level, pressures upon the regime of a very different kind. They were 'unmilitaristic' and arose from the existence of a German industrial proletariat which, although its organizations had been destroyed, nevertheless remained a political force in the Third Reich. It was too large to be ignored and industry was too dependent on its skills. There is a curious discrepancy between the ruthless efficiency with which the Nazis obliterated trade unions and working-class parties after 1933 and their cautious, almost timid treatment of industrial workers as a social group. It seems, as the British historian Tim Mason has argued,[25] that the experience of the First World War and the collapse of the homefront in 1917/18 played a major part in Hitler's velvet-glove approach to the working population. The lesson the Nazis tried to learn from this experience was not to subject the average consumer to material deprivation which might undermine support for their regime. They were convinced — like so many other Germans — that the downfall of the Monarchy in 1918 had been due, not to the military superiority of the Allies, but to the revolutionary 'subversion' and exhaustion of the masses in the rear.

This is the immediate historical background to the guns-*and*-butter policy which Hitler adopted in the 1930s. The regime did not dare to make a choice between maintaining living standards and fully-fledged 'in-depth' rearmament. Instead it pursued a policy which provided *both*, but both, as it turned out, in insufficient quantities. By the late 1930s, the economic effects of the programme of rapid rearmament could be felt. With full employment achieved by 1937, the inflationary spiral began to turn and once again eroded the real income of the industrial workforce and their families. One way of dealing with this potentially dangerous problem would have been to scale back arms production and to step up the manufacture of consumer goods. But this would have weakened further the military back up which the Third Reich needed for its planned territorial expansion. On the other hand, by 1938 the effect of inflation, resulting from the programme of rapid rearmament, began to be reflected in an increasing dissatisfaction on the part of the industrial working class and in particular those skilled workers without whom German industry could not do. This dissatisfaction manifested itself in a growing wave of unofficial strikes, absenteeism and sabotage of machinery which can only be interpreted as evidence of disaffection with a regime whose police state character made other forms of protest impossible. After the hardships of the Great Depression with its large-scale unemployment and short-time work, many German workers may have been willing to accept a dictatorship which, although it had destroyed freedom of expression and association, nevertheless appeared to be looking well after the material interest of the majority of the population.

When after 1936 this was less and less the case, popular loyalty began to fade away, confronting the regime with an insoluble problem. Hitler's escape from this dilemma was to embark upon war in 1939 without, as his generals warned and as the stocktaking of material after the various campaigns demonstrated, being prepared for more than lightning attacks. As early as 1936, even 'armament in breadth', the only programme which the regime had thought it could afford, had reached the limits of Germany's economic possibilities. Thenceforth all systematic planning, which had been the credo of the military technocrats of the Weimar period, collapsed. Organizational chaos and fighting for scarce resources reached new heights, while popular propaganda exhausted itself in exhortations to develop a fighting spirit, but met with little response. Neither mentally nor materially was the Third Reich prepared for total war. Hitler's only hope were swift victories and ruthless exploitation of the conquered territories, if his regime was to survive. His gamble worked initially until, in 1941, he found himself embroiled in a protracted war for which he was technically and industrially unprepared. It is true that Albert Speer, the new Minister for Armaments, succeeded in boosting industrial output after 1942.[26] However, this massive effort still could not match the combined industrial capacity and technological superiority of the Allies. Nor did Joseph Goebbels's total war propaganda succeed in raising the level of spiritual militarism in the mass of the population. By 1945, Nazi Germany lay in ruins, defeated not only by the Soviet Union and the West, but also by its own contradictions.

It should now be possible to put the socio-economic contradictions that undermined the viability of the Third Reich into the broader framework of our analysis of militarism. We argued at the beginning of this chapter that, if related to the economic structures of the society in question, the debate in the first five chapters of this volume revolved in effect around two different types of militarism which the respective authors had in mind. The first type emerged in preindustrial and industrializing societies. It was characterized by the self-exclusiveness of the military sphere, an emphasis on an all-pervasive militaristic spirit to be generated by indoctrination and through large-scale paramilitary organization, and military preparation by means of an austerity programme. The second type is to be found in industrialized high-technology societies. It is marked by a civil-military symbiosis, operating within a predominantly civilian, mass-consumption society and relying on the deterrent value of a push-button nuclear armoury.

Seen in this context, the dilemma of the Nazi regime, which has been analyzed above, demonstrates the point: dating back to the Weimar period, a high-technology militarism had emerged in Germany which reflected and exploited her modern industrial capabilities and state of economic development, but overlapped with the militarism of the *Wehrverbände* of this period. The example of the SA showed how the 'democratic' thrust of Röhm's movement threatened the operations of the military-industrial technocrats. Further doubts arose as to whether it is possible to combine the two types of militarism in a Lasswellian Garrison State, when the problem of the German working class is considered. Given that highly industrialized societies are orientated towards consumption and hence will not bear indefinitely the extended austerity of a society permanently mobilized for total war, the attempt to do both at the same time will prove self-destructive. Since the new 'technological militarism' cannot operate without a skilled workforce which demands material appeasement, the old-style militarism with its reliance on sacrifice and tight discipline becomes counter-productive and tends to jeopardize the stability of the entire system.

There is another way of putting this: the militarism discussed in the first four chapters of this volume is functional only to the type of transitional society with which historians and social scientists have, implicitly or explicitly, associated it. It is dysfunctional to the high-technology societies of East and West after 1945, which are publicly committed to an improvement of living standards and possess total weapons. At a moment in her history when Germany was on the verge of completing the transition and when the constellation of social and economic forces appeared favourable, Hitler may have been dreaming of creating a Lasswellian system, but found its ingredients to be incompatible in practice.

Notes

1   See above, pp. 55ff.
2   For a summary of this tradition see, e.g., O. Butz, *Modern German Political Theory*, New York 1955.
3   G. Ritter, *Staatskunst*, Vol. 1, p.13.
4   S. P. Huntington, *The Soldier and the State*, p.3.
5   See above, pp. 11ff.
6   See above, pp. 26ff.
7   Quoted in J. A. Donovan, *Militarism U.S.A.*, New York 1970, p.25.
8   D. Senghaas, *Rüstung und Militarismus*, pp.11f.
9   See above, pp. 43ff.
10 J. M. Diehl, *Paramilitary Politics*.
11 M. Geyer, 'Der zur Organisation erhobene Burgfriede' in K.-J. Müller and E. Opitz, eds., *Militär und Militarismus in der Weimarer Republik*, Düsseldorf 1978, pp. 15-100. See also G. Post jr., *The Civil-Military Fabric of Weimar Foreign Policy*, Princeton 1973, pp. 346f.
12 See, e.g. F.L. Carsten, *Reichswehr und Politik*, Köln 1964.
13 Quoted in M. Geyer, 'Der zur Organisation erhobene Burgfriede', Ms, 1977, p.48.
14 See also E.W. Hansen, 'Zum "Militärisch-Industriellen Komplex" in der Weimarer Republik' in K.-J. Müller and E. Optiz, eds. *Militär und Militarismus*, pp.101-40. It is significant that Hansen should have chosen to analyse this development in terms of an emergent Military-Industrial Complex.
     K.-J. Müller, *Das Heer und Hitler*, Stuttgart 1969.
16 See, e.g., H. Mommsen, *Beamtentum im Dritten Reich*; R. Bollmus, *Das Amt Rosenberg und seine Gegner*, Stuttgart 1970.
17 See, e.g., B. Klein, *Germany's Economic Preparations for War*, Cambridge (Mass.) 1959.
18 T.W.Mason, *Sozialpolitik im Dritten Reich*, Opladen 1977.
19 E. Ludendorff, *Der totale Krieg*, München 1935, p.5.

20 J. Winschuh, *Männer, Traditionen, Signale*, Berlin 1940, p.319.

21 For details see K. Hildebrand, *The Foreign Policy of the Third Reich*, London 1973, esp.pp. 24ff.

22 A. Hillgruber, *Grossmachtpolitik und Militarismus im 20. Jahrhundert*, Düsseldorf 1974, p.44.

23 R.G.L. Waite, *Vanguard of Nazism. The Free Corps Movement in Postwar Germany*, Cambridge (Mass.) 1952.

24 K.-J. Müller, *Das Heer und Hitler*, pp.88ff.

25 T.W. Mason, *Sozialpolitik*, pp. 15ff. This is one of Mason's central points. But the rest of the argument in this section on National Socialism also relies on his findings ibid., pp.42ff.

26 A. Speer, *Inside the Third Reich*, London 1970, pp.269ff.

Conclusion

We began our survey of the long debate on militarism by arguing that the historical and social sciences would do well to engage in stock-taking exercises of their key concepts from time to time. Subsequent chapters then tried to show how the concept of militarism has been employed during the past century or so as a way of trying to come to terms with a problem which arises in all larger and more complex communities, i.e. the problem of the role and position of the soldier within it.

The first objective of our broadly chronological approach has, naturally, been to reconstruct what various scholars and intellectuals have had to say on this subject. It was hoped that this in itself would be a worthwhile enterprise, if only for two seemingly contradictory reasons. On the one hand, our analysis has revealed how much all writers were constrained in the formulation of ideas by the problem perceptions of their age. By and large, they all theorized about what they saw, or believed to see, around them. Few of them really ventured outside the prevailing intellectual context and into frontier territories of knowledge. On the other hand, there are not many basic arguments in today's debate which have not, in one way or another, been advanced before. The language may be different; the methods may be more sophisticated, but most of the issues were formulated before 1945. It was also not too difficult to extract the crucial point which, directly or indirectly, has preoccupied most writers in the field: the question of the societal structures which gave rise to militarism and then allowed it to persist and even flourish.

There were, it is true, phases in the debate when the systemic aspect receded into the background. Thus the West German discussion on militarism unleashed by Ritter in the 1950s revolved largely around the problem of the 'proper balance' between political and military considerations guiding the decision-making processes of the Prusso-German state. A similar emphasis developed among Anglo-Saxon scholars in the early postwar debate on civil-military relations in developing countries. Recently this particular perspective has again received a certain amount of attention in connection with re-examinations of the role of the American military during various 'Cold War Crises'. But as the example of Betts's study has demonstrated,[1*] the scope of such books is inevitably limited and remains confined to the politics and crisis management aspects of the problem. Other authors, as we have seen, have continued to give priority to the impact, on

the civil-military relationship, of the international system as an ex-
ogenous factor. It is an approach which we were first able to discover
in Hintze's writings at the turn of the century. Significantly enough,
however, the 'primacy of foreign policy' was never his primary concern. Like Spencer and the Marxists, with both of whom he took issue,
Hintze, too, was always more interested in broader systemic questions.
And indeed, even if militarism was initially defined in political terms,
sooner or later a more basic theme would appear on the horizon, i.e.
what is the character of the *society* in which it arises.

It was with reference to this question that a major disagreement
occurred in the late nineteenth century between Liberal theorists and
the Marxists. Given the measure of agreement which, as we have seen,
has developed between these two schools of thought during the past
two decades, the earlier debate may seem puzzling and calls for an
explanation. To be sure, there are still fundamental differences of view
resulting from the divergent teleologies of Liberalism and Marxism.
However, considerable weight must be attached to the fact that both
Liberal and Marxist contributors to the pre-1914 debate on militarism
tended to make the Prusso-German Empire their central reference
point. Since key elements of the early theories were derived from the
observation of agrarian societies, liberal Anglo-Saxon writers moved
on fairly safe ground when ruminating upon the Prussian example. In
their attempt to define the phenomenon of Prussian militarism (and
implicitly also desirous to refute the Marxist critique that Western
capitalist-industrial societies were necessarily militaristic) they
stressed the differences between 'backward' Prussia-Germany and
more advanced West; they pointed to the 'unhealthy' weight of the
Prussian military in political decision-making, to the lack of civilian
control and to the pervasion of society by military values. This was a
viable and perfectly consistent approach.

The early Marxists, on the other hand, were prone to get their
analysis badly wrong when they took Imperial Germany as the paradigm
of a capitalist-industrial militarism. Certain features of 'modernity'
notwithstanding, the Central European monarchy was plainly not a
developed industrial society like Britain. They were therefore really
talking about a militarism of the future while drawing upon the
example of a country whose militarism was more accurately defined by
non-Marxist writers of the time. The weakness of the non-Marxist
approach was that it became fixated on the Prussian case, while the
economies and societies of Europe were undergoing rapid change and
experienced total war. At least it took Western historians and social
scientists a long time to come to terms with the implications of the

'industrialization of war' in the twentieth century which resulted in the bureaucratization and '"industrialization" of the military'.[2] With the possible exception of Lasswell, there was no-one to turn to this particular theme in a systematic way before the 1950s, and even Lasswell, as we have shown, did not mean to apply his analysis of a 'technological militarism' to the West, but appears to have had Nazi Germany in mind.

There was yet another group of contributors to the debate: the intellectual militarists of the interwar period who gathered around Ernst Jünger and who wrote about a future militaristic society which combined the Prussian version of militarism with the industrial one. Their idea was to create a synthesis between what were the (frightening) strengths of Spencer's 'militant society', on the one hand, and the efficiency of a high-technology industrial system. We have seen in Chapter VI above how this fusion failed to work when it was attempted in Hitler's 'totally mobilized' Third Reich. The conclusion to be drawn from our analysis of the policies adopted by the Hitler regime was that there exist two divergent types of militarism. This would place Nazi Germany at the very end of the transitional continuum from an agrarian to an industrial order, partly straddling the dividing line between the two. This image must not be taken too literally. The crucial point is this: if the Third Reich had been an advanced capitalist system, its leaders would not have been able even to contemplate the programme of militarization *in peacetime* which was launched by Hitler in 1933. It seems significant that those who were at the helm of the developed industrial systems of Britain and America in the 1930s never adopted the German recipe. If, on the other hand, the National Socialist system had still been steeped in preindustrial structures, it would hardly have been capable of the technological and organizational effort which was undertaken by the Third Reich in the military field. Nazi militarism was janus-faced and not a product of the 'monopoly stage' of capitalism.[3]

With the disappearance of the Prusso-German stumbling-bloc in the debate on militarism, the path was cleared for a fresh look at Liberal and Marxist interpretations. The result was a gradual rapprochement between the two major schools of thought. However mistaken they may have been in this, for Liebknecht or Luxemburg it would have been inconceivable to view Wilhelmine militarism as anything but a militarism of the capitalist-industrial variety. If one looks at what is now being written by East European Marxists, a differentiated approach is very much in evidence. Thus the East German historians Horst Giertz and Wolfgang Küttler have propounded the view that the

militarism of the transition period from feudalism to capitalism represents a clearly identifiable system which can be delineated from the
'imperialistic militarism' of the advanced capitalist countries.[4] And as
far as the epoch prior to the transitional phase is concerned, it is, they
believe, merely possible to observe 'militaristic tendencies'. It is this
periodization which enables East European historians to engage in an
analysis of Prusso-German militarism similar to that of non-Marxist
Western scholars.

Nor have Western Liberal theorists of militarism stopped there. In
fact they have likewise come a long way since the First World War. To
begin with, although the civil-military relationship continued to command considerable attention, it came to be seen increasingly within the
larger context of the socio-economic structures of the country in
question. Secondly, a growing preoccupation with problems of systems
stability led to an interest in the functionality of militarism. And finally,
the growth of major research industries in the fields of 'civil-military
relations' in the Third World, on the one hand, and of the Military-
Industrial Complex on the other, involved, if nothing else, the tacit
admission that one was in effect dealing with two different militarisms.
It was to be expected that, with the disappearance of the Prussian
object of study in 1945, attention would first turn to the transitional
cases provided by the 'New Nations'. Janowitz, one of the pioneers in
this field, has, together with other sociologists, suggested various
categories of analysis which might by applied with benefit not only to
developing countries of today, but also to the transitional societies of
Central Europe in the period up to 1945.

In his most recent book, Janowitz has investigated 'paramilitarism'
which he feels is a neglected aspect of Third World regimes.[5] Time will
show how far, as he speculated, these paramilitary forces are able to
exert a long-term stabilizing influence on the dictatorships of Latin
America and elsewhere. But more importantly perhaps, if one reads
about the extensive networks of army, police, local defence units and
militias in the developing world, one cannot avoid being reminded of
interwar Europe and, of post-1933 Germany. Janowitz was struck by
this parallel, even if he was reluctant to make direct comparisons
because the regimes of the 'New Nations' are, in his view, far less
'radical' than National Socialism. On the other hand, he left his future
options open when he argued that the transitional countries whose
paramilitarism he has been studying 'have not yet [!] drifted into
becoming fully repressive regimes of the totalitarian type'.[6] Considering that the militarization of the Third World is continuing, we
may indeed wish to wait and see.

Whereas research into the militarism of the 'New Nations' pro-
liferated quite rapidly in the 1950s and 1960s, partly perhaps because it
neatly fitted into a tradition of Western evolutionary thinking which
reappeared after 1945 in the guise of modernization theories, it took
somewhat longer for the 'new militarism' of the advanced industrial
nations to become a matter of scholarly concern. Whatever the carefully maintained barriers may have been that had existed in the West
between civilian society and the military, they had definitely begun to
collapse with the advent of missiles and nuclear weapons as well as the
growing organization and bureaucratization of the high-technology
countries. After 1945, the '"industrialization" of the military', which
had been ushered in by the First World War, was at first conceptualized
in terms of the professionalization of the soldier.[7] But the debate soon
broadened to include an examination of the 'defense intellectuals', the
'civilian militarists' and the coalition of powerful groups which were
assumed to make up the Military-Industrial Complex. Their social
composition, organizational leverage and outlook is now being investigated as well. The same applied to the position and role of armed
forces in the Soviet Union. Whatever one may think about the disagreements between Jahn, Kolkowicz, Colton and Odom,[8] there is
little in their writings to suggest that Russia is to be seen as a
praetorian, rather than an industrial society.

There may have been a time when 'militarism', because of its
shrill political overtones, did not appear to be particularly useful to
academic discussion. The emergence of a greater consensus about
what it might be, on the other hand, would make it seem unwise to
discard the concept now. We do not possess, it is true, an agreed theory
of militarism. This is a reflection of the fact that there are also 'no great
theories of violence, as there are theories of social stratification and
culture'.[9] Indeed, our understanding of the problem of violence,
whether legal or illegal, in human society is still quite primitive.[10]
However, there appears to be room for agreement of a more modest
kind: on a typology which distinguishes between a militarism of pre-
industrial and industrializing societies and that of high-technology
industrial systems orientated towards and pledged to, mass consumption. Future work will obviously have to test the argument presented in
Chapter VI further.[11] More information will also be required about
civil-military relations at different stages of a particular country's
history.[12] However chilling this thought may be, the future may also
show that someone will succeed where the Nazis failed and create a
stable 'Garrison State'. At the moment it is difficult to imagine how the
divergent imperatives of Jüngerian society could be reconciled. It

seems more likely that one day we may be studying a militarism of a third type: that of a computerized post-industrial no-growth society — its 'guardians' permitting.

Notes

1 See above, pp. 94f.
2 M. Geyer, 'Die Geschichte des deutschen Militärs von 1860 bis 1945' in H.-U. Wehler, ed., *Die moderne deutsche Geschichte in der internationalen Forschung, 1945-1975*, Göttingen 1978, p.264.
3 This merely by way of cross-reference to the lively debate on the basic character of German Fascism. See the survey by W. Wippermann, *Faschismustheorien*, Darmstadt 1975. See also W.Z. Laqueur, ed., *Fascism*, London 1976; E.J. Weber, *Varieties of Fascism*, Englewood Cliffs 1964.
4 H. Giertz and W. Küttler, 'Zur Inhaltsbestimmung und historischen Dimension des Militarismusbegriffs.' *Militärgeschichte* 15 (1976), pp.407-17.
5 M. Janowitz, *Military Institutions and Coercion in Developing Nations*, Chicago 1977, pp.3ff.
6 Ibid., p.73.
7 See, e.g., M. Janowitz, *The Professional Soldier*, Glencoe 1961.
8 See above pp. 97ff.
9 M. Janowitz, *Military Institutions*, p.17.
10 Work on this subject received a major stimulus through the emergence of Peace and Conflict Research as a new discipline. The argument has been further enlivened, though not become clearer, by the discussion on 'structural violence' as well as on the 'counter-violence' of urban guerilla movements. It is one of the weaknesses of this book that it did not dare to plunge into these deep waters.
11 Israel may be posing particularly interesting questions in terms of the above analysis. Amos Perlmutter has, in the past ten years, undertaken two studies on the subject (*Military and Politics in Israel*, London 1969; *Politics and the Military in Israel, 1967-1977*, London 1978). The first book asked the then customary questions (civil-military relations; praetorianism; 'nation-building') and came to the conclusion that civilian dominance was assured and that Israel was not a praetorian state. It was also not a Lasswellian Garrison State, though he did use the term 'Garrisoned State' (pp.119, 135). In Israel itself many people seem to agree that they live in a militarized society, but not in a militaristic one. However, there is also the more sceptical assessment by the journalist M. Woollacott, 'The Tunnel Vision of Endless Wars' *The Guardian*, 30.5.1979.
12 Very interesting work is now being done on nineteenth-century Prussia by Alf Lüdtke. See his 'Militärstaat und "Festungspraxis" ' in V.R. Berghahn, *Militarismus*, pp. 164-85.

Bibliography

This bibliography contains English-language publications only on the topics covered by this book. Full bibliographical references on foreign-language texts are to be found in the footnotes. It was felt that the adoption of this principle would be more helpful to the reader in that it provides an extended bibliography which, because of the exclusion of foreign-language texts cited, is not excessively long.

Abrahamson, B. *Military Professionalisation and Political Power*. London 1972.

Andrzejewski (now Andreski), S. *Military Organisation and Society*. London 1954.

Angel, N. *The Great Illusion*. London 1911.

Aspaturian, V.V. 'The Soviet Military-Industrial Complex — Does It Exist?' *Journal of International Affairs* 26 (1972) : 1-28.

Awe, B. 'Militarism and Economic Development in Ninteenth-Century Yoruba Country: the Example of Ibadan.' *Journal of African History* 14 (1973): 65-77.

Barnes, J. C. M. *The Soldier in Modern Society*. London 1972.

Barnet, R. J. *The Economy of Death*. New York 1969.

Benoit, E. *Defense and Economic Growth in Developing Countries*. Lexington (Mass.) 1973.

Betts, R. K. *Soldiers, Statesmen and Cold War Crises*. Cambridge (Mass.) 1977.

Bienen, H., ed. *The Military Intervenes*. New York 1968.

——, *Armies and Parties in Africa*. New York 1978.

Bosch, J. *Pentagonism. A Substitute for Imperialism*. New York 1969.

Bram, J. *Analysis of Inca Militarism*. New York 1941.

Brotz, H., and Wilson, E.K. 'Characteristics of Military Society.' *American Journal of Sociology* 51 (1946) : 371ff.

Carsten, F. L. *The Reichswehr and Politics*. London 1965.

Causton, E. *Militarism and Foreign Policy in Japan*. London 1936.

Challener, R. D. *The French Theory of the Nation in Arms, 1866-1939*. New York 1965.

——, *Admirals, Generals and American Foreign Policy, 1898-1914*. Princeton 1973

Chickering, R. *Imperial Germany and a World Without War*. Princeton 1975.

Coffin, T. *The Passion of the Hawks. Militarism in Modern America*, New York 1964.

Colgrove, K. W. *Militarism in Japan*. Boston-New York 1936.

Colton, T. J. *Commissars, Commanders and Civilian Authority*. Cambridge (Mass.) 1979.

Cook, F. J. *The Warfare State*. New York 1962.

Craig, G. *The Politics of the Prussian Army, 1640-1945*. Oxford 1955.

Cunliffe, M. *Soldiers and Civilians*. London 1969.

Dibble, V.K. 'The Garrison Society.' *New University Thought* 5 (1966/67):Special Issue.

Diehl, J. M. *Paramilitary Politics in Weimar Germany*.Bloomington 1977.

Donovan, J. A. *Militarism U.S.A.* New York 1970.

Doorn, J. van, ed. *Armed Forces and Society*. Den Haag-Paris 1968.

——, ed. *Military Profession and Military Regimes*. Den Haag-Paris 1969.

Ekirch, A. A. *The Civilian and the Military*. New York 1956.

Enloe, C. N., and Semin-Panzer, U., eds. *The Military, the Police and Domestic Order*. London 1976.

Erickson, J. *The Soviet High Command*. London 1962.

Feit, E. 'Military Coups and Political Development: Some Lessons from Ghana and Nigeria.' *World Politics* 10 (1968): 179-93.

Ferrero, G. *Militarism*. London 1902.

Fidel, K., ed. *Militarism in Developing Countries*. New Brunswick 1975.

Finer, S. E. *The Man on Horseback*. London 1962.

Fulbright, J. W. *The Pentagon Propaganda Machine*. New York 1970.

Galbraith, J. K. *How to Control the Military*. New York 1969.

Gilbert, F., ed. *The Historical Essays of Otto Hintze*. New York 1975.

Gilmore, R. *Caudilism and Militarism in Venezuela, 1810-1910*. Athens (Ohio) 1964.

Gutteridge, W. *Armed Forces in New States*. London 1962.

Hamer, W. S. *The British Army. Civil-Military Relations, 1885-1905*. Oxford 1970.

Hersprings, D., and Volgyes, I., eds. *Civil-Military Relations in Communist Systems*. Boulder 1978.

Horowitz, I. L. *The War Game. Studies on the New Civilian Militarists*. New York 1963.

Howard, M. *Soldiers and Governments*. London 1957.

Huntington, S.P. *The Soldier and the State*. Cambridge (Mass.) 1957.

——, ed. *Changing Patterns of Military Politics*. New York 1962.

——, *Political Order in Changing Societies*, New Haven 1968.

Jackman, R. W. 'Politicians in Uniform: Military Governments and Social Change in the Third World.' *American Political Science Review* 70 (1976): 1078-97.

Janowitz, M. *The Professinal Soldier*. Glencoe 1961.

——, *The Military in the Political Development of New Nations*. Chicago 1964.

——, *Military Institutions and Coercion in Developing Nations*. Chicago 1977.

——, and Doorn, J. van, eds. *On Military Intervention*. Rotterdam 1971.

Johnson, J. J. *The Military and Society in Latin America*. Stanford 1964.

——, ed. *The Role of the Military in Underdeveloped Countries*. Princeton 1968.

Kaufman, R. F. *The War Profiteers*. Indianapolis 1970.

Kehr, E. *Economic Interest, Militarism and Foreign Policy*. Stanford 1977.

Kelleher, C. M., ed. *Political-Military Systems: Comparative Perspectives*. Beverly Hills 1974.

Kennedy, G. *The Military in the Third World*. London 1974.

Kennedy, M. D. *The Military Side of Japanese Life*. London 1924.

Kitchen, M. *The German Officer Corps*. Oxford 1968.

Klein, B. *Germany's Economic Preparations for War*. Cambridge (Mass.) 1959.

Knoll, E., and McFadden, J. N., eds. *American Militarism*. New York 1969.

Koistinen, P. 'The Military-Industrial Complex in Historical Perspective: the Interwar Years.' Journal of American History 55 (1970): 819-39.

Kolkowicz, R. *The Soviet Military and the Communist Party*. Princeton 1967.

Land, G., ed. *Military Institutions and the Sociology of War*. London 1972.

Lapp, R. W. *The Weapons Culture*. New York 1968.

Lasswell, H. D. 'The Sino-Japanese Crisis: the Garrison State vs. the Civilian State.' *China Quarterly* 2 (1937): 643-49.

——, 'The Garrison State and the Specialists on Violence.' *American Journal of Sociology* 47 (1941): 455-68.

Lauterbach, A. 'Militarism in the Western World.' *Journal of the History of Ideas* 5 (1944): 446-78.

Lee, J. M. *African Armies and Civil Order*. London 1969.

Lee, W. 'The Politico-Military Complex of the USSR.' *Journal of International Affairs* 26 (1972): 73-86.

Lefever, E. W. *Spear and Scepter: Army, Police and Politics in Tropical Africa*. Washington 1970.

Lens, S. *The Military-Industrial Complex*. Philadelphia 1970.

Lewy, G. *America in Vietnam*. New York 1978.

Lieberson, S. 'An Empirical Study of Military-Industrial Linkages.' *American Journal of Sociology* 76 (1970): 562-84.

Lieuwen, E. *Generals vs. Presidents. Neo-Militarism in Latin America*. New York 1964.

Lissak, M. *Military Roles in Modernization: Civil-Military Relations in Thailand and Burma*. Beverly Hills 1976.

Luckham, A. R. *The Nigerian Army*. Cambridge 1971.

——, 'A Comparative Typology of Civil-Military Relations.' *Government and Opposition* 6 (1971) : 5-35.

——, 'Militarism.' *IDS-Bulletin* 8 (1977): 38-50.

——, 'Militarism.' *IDS-Bulletin* 9 (1977) : 19-32.

Luxemburg, R. *Accumulation of Capital*. London 1951.

McWilliams, W., ed. *Garrisons and Governments*. San Francisco 1967.

Magdoff, H. 'Militarism and Imperialism.' *American Economic Review* 60 (1970): 237-42 (Papers and Proceedings).

Maki, J. M. *Japanese Militarism*. New York 1945.

Maruyama, M. *Thought and Behaviour of Modern Japanese Politics*. Oxford 1969.

Maxon, Y. C. *Control of Japanese Foreign Policy*. Berkeley 1957.

Meinecke, F. *The German Catastrophe*. New York 1963.

Melman, S. *Pentagon Capitalism*. New York 1970.

Mills, C. W. *The Power Elite*. New York 1956.

Morris, A. J. A. *Radicalism Against War*. London 1972.

Morris, I., ed. *Japan 1931-1945. Militarism, Fascism, Japanism?* Boston 1963.

Needler, M. C. 'The Latin American Military : Predatory Reactionaries or Modernizing Patriots?' *Journal of Inter-American Studies* 11 (1969): 237-44.

——, *The United States and the Latin American Revolution*. Boston 1972.

Nef, J. U. *War and Human Progress*. Cambridge (Mass.) 1950.

Nelson, K. L. *The Impact of War on Life*. New York 1971.

Nordlinger, E. A. 'Soldiers in Mufti.' *American Political Science Review* 56 (1970): 1131ff.

——, *Soldiers in Politics*. Englewood Cliffs (N. J.) 1977.

North, L. *Civil-Military Relations in Argentina, Chile and Peru*. Berkeley 1966.

Özbudun, E. *The Role of the Military in Recent Turkish Politics*. Cambridge (Mass.) 1966.

O'Neill, R. *The German Army and the Nazi Party*. London 1966.

Otley, C. B. 'Militarism and Militarisation in the Public Schools, 1900-1972.' *British Journal of Sociology* 29 (1978) : 3231-39.

Perlmutter, A. 'The Praetorian State and the Praetorian Army.' *Comparative Politics* 1 (1969) : 382-404.

——, *The Military and Politics in Israel*. London 1969.

——, *The Military and Politics in Modern Times*. New Haven 1977.

——, *Politics and the Military in Israel, 1967-1977*. London 1977.

Pilisuk, M., and Hayden, T. 'Is There a Military-Industrial Complex Which Prevents Peace?' *Journal of Social Issues* 21 (1965) : 67-117.

Post, G. *The Civil-Military Fabric of Weimar Foreign Policy*. Princeton 1973.

Proxmire, W. *Report From Wasteland*. New York 1970.

Pursell, C. W. jr., ed. *The Military-Industrial Complex*. New York 1972.

Relston, D. B. *The Army of the Republic*. Cambridge (Mass.) 1967.

Ritter, G. *The Sword and the Sceptre. The Problem of 'Militarism' in Germany*. 4 vols. London 1972ff.

Rosen, S., ed. *Testing the Theory of the Military-Industrial Complex*. Teakfield 1973.

Russett, B. M., and Stepan, A. C., eds. *Military Force and American Society*. New York 1973.

Sarkesian, S. C. *The Military-Industrial Complex: A Reassessment*. London 1973.

Schiller, H., and Phillips, J., eds. *Superstate. Readings in the Military-Industrial Complex*. Urbana 1970.

Schmitter, P. C., ed. *Military Rule in Latin America. Function, Consequences and Perspectives*. Berverly Hills-London 1973.

Shoup, D. M. 'The New American Militarism.' *The Atlantic Monthly* 223 (1969) : 51-56.

Smaldone, J. P. 'Military Rule in Africa: Roots, Results and Ramifications.' *Current Bibiliography on African Affairs* 11 (1978/79) : 110-14.

Smethurst, R.J. *A Social Basis for Prewar Japanese Militarism*. Berkeley 1974.

Smith, M. *Militarism and Statecraft*. New York-London 1918.

Spencer, H. *Principles of Sociology*. Vol. II/2, New York-London 1886.

Stepan, A. *The Military in Politics: Changing Patterns in Brazil*. Princeton 1971.

——, *The State and Society: Peru in Comparative Perspective*. Princeton 1978.

Tanin, O., and Yohan, E. *Militarism and Fascism in Japan*. London 1934 (1973).

Thayer, G. *The War Business*. New York 1969.

Thomas, R. H. *Militarism Or Military Fever. Its Causes, Dangers, Cure*. Philadelphia 1899.

Thompson, M. 'Militarism 1969. A Survey of World Trends.' *Peace Research News* 5 (1968) : 1-96.

Toynbee, A. *War and Civilisation*. London 1951.

Vagts, A. *A History of Militarism. Romance and Realities of a Profession*. London 1938.

Ward, R., and Rustow, D., *Political Modernization in Japan and Turkey*. Princeton 1964.

Warner III, E. L. *The Military in Contemporary Soviet Politics*, New York 1977.

Weigley, R. F., ed. *The American Military*. Reading (Mass.) 1969.

Wheeler-Bennett, J. *The Nemesis of Power*. London 1953.

Williams, W. E. 'Paramilitarism in Inter-State Relations. The Role of Political Armies in Twenthieth-Century Politics.' PhD. dissertation, University of London, 1965.

Wolpin, M.D. 'Marx and the Radical Militarism in the Developing Nations.' *Armed Forces and Society* 4 (1978) : 245-65.

Wood, D. *The Armed Forces of the African States*. London 1966.

Yarmolinski, A. *The Military Establishment*. New York 1971.

Index